Why They Must Go:

A Biblical Mandate for Seventh-day Adventist Christian Education

TERRELL MCCOY

iUniverse, Inc.
Bloomington

Why They Must Go
A Biblical Mandate for Seventh-day Adventist Christian Education

iUniverse books may be ordered through booksellers or by contacting:

iUniverse
1663 Liberty Drive
Bloomington, IN 47403
www.iuniverse.com
1-800-Authors (1-800-288-4677)

ISBN: 978-1-4502-7300-8 (sc)
ISBN: 978-1-4502-7301-5 (ebook)

Library of Congress Control Number: 2010916939

Printed in the United States of America

iUniverse rev. date: 12/29/2010

To my darling wife Beverly and the host of other unsung heroes committed to the ministry of teaching in Seventh-day Adventist schools.

Acknowledgments

Special thanks to my wife Beverly and our children, Chavvah, Martin, and Terrell Jr., and to Dr. Daniel Amfo, Elder Donald Bedney, Elder E. C. Polite, Mrs. Shakuntala Ramsarran, Dr. Penny Lister-Smith, Dr. Doug Walker, Dr. Eunice Warfield, Elder Bill Winston, and Elder B. E. Wright for their words of encouragement, proofreading, prayers, and helpful suggestions in regard to this project.

Table of Contents

INTRODUCTION

Doug Walker, the education director for the Southwestern Union of Seventh-day Adventists, gave a sobering presentation on the state of the schools in our union. Although K–12 enrollment was up slightly for the 2007–2008 school year, enrollment trends were far from positive. While the Southwestern Union Conference membership increased over the past decade and a half by a most gratifying 63 percent and the number of churches grew from 491 to 543, school enrollment remained almost static. Of the 123 schools that had operated during this time, only 62 remained in operation.

As a new member of the Southwestern Union's executive committee, I listened intently. From my previous experience as a pastor in central Arkansas, I knew firsthand the strain of pastoring a church with a school that stayed in the academic intensive care unit. Code Blue was called several times as our emaciated school in Little Rock struggled to keep operating. Desperate cries went out on many occasions for transfusions of cash and students.

How and why was an active, growing church like ours experiencing a decline in enrollment and facing closure? We had more than enough children in our congregation to fill our school. My daily prayer was, "What can I do as a pastor? How do I reverse this dire predicament in my part of God's vineyard? Lord, what do you want me to do?"

From my perspective, our members didn't comprehend the vast depth of their calling in Christ Jesus and the implications it had for them, their entire families, and future generations. As I prayed for a solution to the declining enrollment, I resolved to preach sermons on Christian education for the entire month of January every year as long as I pastored that church. I did that for the next four years. This book is an outgrowth of that sermon series.

Some believe that the increase in the cost of Adventist education has caused the decline in enrollment of our schools. I respectfully disagree. And yet, we should do all in our power to provide affordable education to our membership.

I am convinced that when people really understand the vitality of an enterprise, their support, financial and otherwise, follows. If they know better, they do better. On this point, I agree with the German philosopher Friedrich Nietzsche who said, "He who has a strong enough *why* can bear almost any *how.*" One preacher puts it this way: "Vision precedes provision." If we wholeheartedly embrace God's vision for educating His young people, then money and resources will flow to make it a reality.

The following pages seek to make plain God's purpose in establishing the Adventist educational system. May this book be used by the Almighty to strenghten the support of Adventist schools by Adventist members. I also pray that this book will reenergize our church and school administrators to stay the course in keeping the "church" in our church schools.

From God's Perspective

God's Property: They Don't Belong To You

I heard a knock at my dorm room door in the spring of 1973. There stood Roger, a new transfer student from the U.S. Military Academy at West Point. Roger asked to borrow my handheld blow-dryer. (We wore our hair in big Afros back then.) "Sure, no problem," I replied.

Thirty minutes later, he returned with my blow-dryer in two pieces. Roger accidentally broke it. We've been friends for over thirty-five years, and he doesn't even remember this incident. Unfortunately, I do because he broke something that belonged to me.

My mother taught me to take good care of other people's property. "Try," she said, "to return it to them in better condition than you received it." I've tried to follow this advice throughout the years, especially in my role as a father of two children. In the whole scheme of things, breaking the blow-dryer was not a big deal. But, what a shame if we broke or destroyed something that belongs to God!

Throughout the sacred scriptures, the Bible emphasizes God's ownership of all creation—especially people. The Lord declares, "If I were hungry, I would not tell thee: for the world is mine, and the fullness thereof" (Psalms 50:12). And again, "Lo, children are an heritage of the LORD: and the fruit of the womb is his reward" (Psalms 127:3). And finally, "Behold, all souls are mine; as the soul of the father, so also the soul of the son is mine" (Ezekiel 18:4).

Based upon the solid testimony of scripture, Bible-believing Christians understand that children are God's property. They don't belong to us. No wonder Jesus bids us to pray, "Our *Father*." God is our father, not our grandfather or great-grandfather.

We belong to God twice: by creation and by redemption. The God of the universe claims us as His because He created us in His own image and likeness. Moreover, after mankind fell into sin, the God who created us became our Redeemer through Jesus Christ, who died on Calvary for the remission of our sins.

> "Children are the heritage of the Lord, and we are answerable to Him for our management of His property … In love, faith, and prayer let parents work for their households, until with joy they can come to God saying, 'Behold, I and the children whom the Lord hath given me.'"[1]

> "Children derive life and being from their parents, and yet it is through the creative power of God that your children have life, for God is the Life-giver. Let it be remembered that children are not to be treated as though they were our own personal property. Children are the heritage of the Lord, and the plan of redemption includes their salvation as well as ours. They have been entrusted to parents in order that they might be brought *up in the nurture and admonition of the Lord*, that they might be *qualified to do their work in time and eternity*."[2]

Once we accept this basic premise, that children are God's property and they don't belong to us, then we must relate to them God's way.

Here are three basic ways to relate to children as property of the Almighty.

1.   Treat Them with Dignity.

We should show respect to all of God's creation, including the environment and animals and particularly human beings, who are created in His image. Children are human beings, and we have no right to abuse and misuse our little ones because we are bigger, stronger, smarter, and more experienced than they are.

While leaving a supermarket one day, I overheard a young woman arguing with her four-year-old son. The tiny lad didn't get a treat that his little heart desperately desired and began to throw a mild temper tantrum. This young mother proceeded to give him a severe tongue-lashing, which included many curse words that I dare not repeat. Is this treating God's creation with respect? Is this according to the will of God? What does such behavior say to our Creator?

Fearful are the words recorded in Matthew 18:6, 10: "But whoso shall offend one of these little ones which believe in me, it were better for him that a millstone were hanged about his neck, and that he were drowned in the depth of the sea ... Take heed that ye despise not one of these little ones; for I say unto you, That in heaven their angels do always behold the face of my Father which is in heaven."

A church member is thinking, "I don't curse my children. I don't beat my children mercilessly. I don't abuse and misuse God's property." To which I reply, "Hallelujah! Praise the Lord!" But, is it possible to abuse our young people in the area of education? Is it possible to mistreat God's property because we do not provide them with an Adventist education?

Listen to the solemn words of the prophet recorded in Ezekiel 16:20–21: "Moreover thou hast taken thy sons and thy daughters, whom thou hast borne unto me, and these hast thou sacrificed unto them to be devoured. Is this of thy whoredoms a small matter, that thou hast slain my children, and delivered them to cause them to pass through the fire for them?" Note that God claims ownership of the children. He emphatically states that they were borne unto *Him* and that the people slew *His* children.

The children of Israel engaged in the practice of idol worship and openly sacrificed their sons and daughters to heathen gods such as Baal, Moloch, and Chemosh. They burnt their offspring alive to plead the favor of nonliving deities. And again you say, "I'd never do that to my children. I love them too much. I wouldn't do anything to harm them." Is it any less harmful if we send our youth to schools that teach contrary to His Word? Are we not—figuratively and unsuspectingly—sacrificing our sons and daughters to idol gods when we send them to institutions that seek to destroy their faith in the Bible and its Author?

A retired public school teacher shared with me that three sets of lesbian parents had children in her classroom during her last year of teaching. One of these parents happened to be the PTA president. What messages are we sending to our boys and girls in these situations?

With so many ungodly things transpiring in public school, can we honestly say that we are treating our young people with dignity when we enroll them in these schools? And for those who send their youth to Christian schools that teach them it is all right to disobey *one* of God's Ten Commandments[3], is this not also ill treatment of our offspring? Can we place them in environments hostile to their faith at such a vulnerable and formative time in their lives and truly claim to be treating them with the respect they deserve and the care God demands?

Undoubtedly, the education of our heirs plays a vital part in recognizing them as God's property. It is impossible to treat them with dignity while disregarding what, where, how, and by whom they are taught.

2.   Train Them with Diligence.

The recognition of God as the owner of our sons and daughters demands that we not only treat our children with dignity, but that we also train them with diligence. Anything God owns and entrusts to our care requires more than our fleeting attention. Exercising persevering diligence in training our young ones is the right and sensible thing to do. Remember, we *are* talking about God's property. They don't belong to us. Besides, the Lord has repeatedly commanded us to do so.

The Lord wants us to cooperate with Him in *diligently* teaching and training our little ones for Him. Deuteronomy 4:9 states, "Only take heed to yourself, and *diligently* keep yourself, lest you forget the things your eyes have seen, and lest they depart from your heart all the days of your life. And *teach them to your children and your grandchildren.*" This text emphasizes our need to *diligently* keep ourselves in the faith and closes by admonishing us to pass our faith on to our children and grandchildren. Though this particular text doesn't specifically say it, God's plan is for us to *diligently* teach and train our descendants in *His* ways.

This objective is more forcefully stated in Deuteronomy 6:7–9, in which God commands, "You shall teach them *diligently* to your children, and shall talk of them when you sit in your house, when you walk by the way, when you lie down, and when you rise up. You shall bind them as a sign on your hand, and they shall be as frontlets between your eyes. You shall write them on the doorposts of your house and on your gates."

The Hebrew word for *diligently* in this verse means "to prick" or "to pierce." God expects us to be persistent in transmitting truth to our kids so that it will get through to them. While growing up, my mom sometimes accused my friends, siblings, and me of being "hardheaded." Some of our kids appear to be "hardheaded," stubborn, and impenetrable when it comes to the truths of God's Word. The Lord knows this and instructs us to be "*diligent*" in our training and teaching of our little ones.

This verse also implies that the *timing* of our teaching is an essential component of being diligent in training our youth. The time to teach our boys and girls about God is *all the time* if we are truly going to be diligent about this task. There's *never* a time when we are not teaching our young people about the Master. This is why God admonishes us to teach them "when we sit in our house, walk, lie down, and rise up." We are encouraged to live so that God's messages are exemplified in our daily lives. The truth of God's Word is to be so real in our lives that it *appears* to our children that God's laws are actually written upon our bodies and upon the very gates and doors of our homes.

> "The education and training of their children to be Christians is the highest service that parents can render to God. It is a work that demands patient labor, a lifelong *diligent* and persevering effort. By a neglect of this trust we prove ourselves unfaithful stewards. No excuse for such neglect will be accepted by God."[4]

In Isaiah 54:13, the prophet writes, "And *all* thy children shall be taught of the LORD; and great shall be the peace of thy children." In

Psalms 78:5–7, we find these words: "For he established a testimony in Jacob, and appointed a law in Israel, which he commanded our fathers, that they should make them known to their children: That the generation to come might know them, even the children which should be born; who should arise and declare them to their children: That they might set their hope in God, and not forget the works of God, but keep his commandments:"

If we send our youth to public schools, can we truthfully say that *all* our children are *diligently* taught of the Lord? If we send them to Christian schools that do not believe in keeping all of God's Ten Commandments, do not have a vital understanding of last-day events, and do not have a proper understanding of how the law and the gospel relate, are we really training our little ones with the *diligence* He has commanded?

3.   Trust Them with the Divine.

Some parents are asking, "What difference does all this really make? We treated our children with dignity. We trained them with diligence. Our kids have only attended Seventh-day Adventist schools all of their lives. Now, they have left the church and are living ungodly lives."

It is always tragic to hear such reports. But this brings me to my third point. In recognizing that children are God's property, we must not only treat them with dignity and train them with diligence, but we must also trust them with the divine.

The Allstate Insurance Company has two great slogans which I'm sure you know: "You're in good hands with Allstate" and "Allstate: the good hands people." I am not seeking to promote this insurance company, just the mighty God that we serve. I proclaim before all that "Our children are in good hands with Jehovah. Jehovah is the good hands God."

After we have done all God has asked of us, we must leave our sons and daughters in the hands of One who loves them infinitely more than we ever could. We must trust God when He exclaims, "So shall my word be that goeth forth out of my mouth: it shall not return unto me void, but it shall accomplish that which I please and prosper in the thing whereto I sent it" (Isaiah 55:11). We have planted the Word of God in our children's lives like precious seed. We have planted and watered, but only God can give the increase. We trust Him to cause an actual seed to grow in the earth; this same trust is needed as we await the spiritual seed to grow in our children's hearts and lives.

Trust God when He announces in Psalms 126:6, "He that goeth forth and weepeth, bearing precious seed, shall doubtless come again with rejoicing, bringing his sheaves with him." Believe His precious promise found in Isaiah 49:25, "But thus saith the LORD, Even the captives of the mighty shall be taken away, and the prey of the terrible shall be delivered: for I will contend with him that contendeth with thee, and *I will save thy children*." Beloved, God loves our children more than we do and is doing everything possible short of violating their free will to bring them to salvation.

Everyone thought that Charles was a lost cause. His mother, a church member, sent him to the local Adventist school at age nine. He attended there through the eighth grade. Unfortunately, somewhere along the way he fell in with the wrong crowd. He became extremely streetwise with a hard-core exterior. His very look would frighten the most timid among us.

Nevertheless, he had a praying mother. She believed in God's power to save her child and continued to send up prayers for him daily. I was thoroughly and pleasantly shocked to hear that Charles was back in church and leading out in a youth revival as one of the main speakers as a young adult in his early thirties.

I would love to tell you that every wayward son and daughter will return to the fold of God before it is too late. But I can't say that with much conviction. What I can say with the utmost of conviction is that God does everything in His power to orchestrate circumstances to persuade His prodigal sons and daughters to return home before probation closes for them.

I shared with a dear friend my concern for our son who was making some wrong decisions at the time. He assured me that we had placed "hooks" in our son by how we raised him. My friend was referring to the "hooks" of daily family devotion, a consistent weekly worship of the Sovereign Lord in corporate worship on God's holy Sabbath day, the Pathfinder Club, youth congresses and federations, sixteen years of Adventist education, and godly examples lived before our son. He told me that God uses these hooks to pull him back to the path of righteousness. "Terrell," he said, "you and Beverly have put something in him that God can use to draw him back. You all have put hooks in him!"

Beloved, when we give our children the benefits of an Adventist education, we put hooks in them. God uses these hooks to draw them back into the fold.

Let's follow our heavenly Father's instructions regarding our children. Treat them with dignity. Train them with diligence. And after we have done all in our power to cooperate with Him for the salvation of our children, let's trust them with the divine.

Discussion Questions

1. Do you agree that our children are God's property and they don't belong to us? Why or why not?

2. Can you think of other implications of accepting this truth (that children are God's property) in addition to what the author mentioned?

3. Do you believe that we can properly relate to our children as God's property and still send them to public school? Why or why not?

4. Do you believe that our children's education plays a vital role in training them diligently for the Lord? Why or why not?

5. What more can you do to be more diligent in the training of your children? Or if you have no children that are school age, does the Lord expect you to assist those in the household of faith who do have children?

Glory, Glory, Glory! The Purpose of Adventist Education

Consider the following statistics taken from the American Academy of Pediatrics and the American Psychological Association. By the time the average child enters junior high school, he or she will have witnessed at least eight thousand murders[5] and more than one hundred thousand other acts of violence on television. By age eighteen, the average young person will have viewed approximately two hundred thousand acts of violence just on television.[6] This number increases as we add other acts of violence from video games and music lyrics, which have become increasingly graphic.

More than one thousand scientific studies and reviews have concluded that significant exposure to media violence increases the risk of aggressive behavior in certain children and adolescents, and desensitizes them to violence.[7] Or to put it another way, it leads our kids away from God, away from knowing Him, and away from reflecting His image.

A typical teen watching TV for one year is exposed to nearly fourteen thousand sexual references[8] with the overwhelming majority referring to sex outside marriage. Such overexposure to sex as presented before today's youth only leads to dire consequences.

Surely, the enemy of our souls does everything in his power to obliterate the knowledge of God in the earth and to make sin appear enticing, pervasive, and normal. He directs an onslaught and bombardment of evil toward our progeny. This calls for a more *diligent* training of our descendants in the ways of the Lord than ever before. Here is where Adventist education comes in. Effort, diligence, and consistency are needed on our part to introduce our young men and women to Jesus as Lord and Savior.

The devil's strategy is to transform humanity into looking and acting like him. That's why he keeps before us glorified images of illicit sex, violence, gross materialism, and idolatry. He knows that by beholding these negative influences we become changed. He is aware that if we look at, listen to, and think about sin long enough, we will become ensnared in its tangled web of lies, deceit, and false promises.

God's Goal

Likewise, our heavenly Father knows that as we behold Him in all of His beauty, glory, and truth, we'll become changed into His image. This happens as we enter into an intimate and personal relationship with the Almighty. Our schools are established to keep this relationship before our boys and girls as their highest privilege in life. Our teachers introduce our children to Jesus, aid them in their walk with Him, and facilitate their growth in Him.

In the beginning, God created the whole earth full of His glory. And thus it was at the end of the creation week, when God saw all that He had made, "and behold, it was very good" (Genesis 1:31). Sin now blights this earth. Yet our Father is not deterred from His original goal of having this planet filled with His glory. Here are just a few scriptures that attest to this fact:

> "And blessed be his glorious name for ever: and let the whole earth be filled with his glory; Amen, and Amen" (Psalms 72:19).

> "For the earth shall be filled with the knowledge of the glory of the LORD, as the waters cover the sea" (Habakkuk 2:14).

> "But as truly as I live, all the earth shall be filled with the glory of the LORD" (Numbers 14:21).

God is determined to use our families to fill the whole earth with His glory. The scripture states that heaven and earth declare the glory of God. And they do. But nothing gives glory to God like one created in His image. After each day of creation, the Bible states that God saw that it was good. It was only after man was created on the sixth day that the Bible pictures God as exclaiming, "Behold, it is very good!"

God's goal is to have all the inhabitants of this world reflect His image, walk in righteousness, and bring glory and praise to Him through their thoughts, words, and deeds. Satan's goal is directly opposite of God's. He craves to see this planet and the entire universe poisoned with iniquity, lawlessness, and unrighteousness. Since the devil led our first parents into sin, he has managed to infest this planet with sin and sinners. Every human being that has been born since Adam and Eve, with the exception of Christ Jesus, has been "born in sin and shaped in iniquity."

Yet this earth will one day be filled with God's glory. The plan of salvation is the great antidote to this world's malignancy of sin. Jesus' death on Calvary is sufficient to reclaim and restore every fallen child of Adam who puts his or her trust in Him. Here again is why Adventist education is so important. The truths of God's Word must inoculate our sons and daughters as they daily behold Him in all of their lessons and do not lose sight of the God who is love. By beholding God's goodness, wisdom, graciousness, and mercy in all of their lessons, they are changed into His image.

The counteracting of our children's natural tendencies to sin will not just happen automatically. They daily face temptations that incessantly beckon them to indulge every lust of the flesh, every lust of the eye, and every prideful, ego-inflating impulse. As parents, we must be *intentional* in our pursuit to cooperate with God for the salvation of our heirs. Plans must be well laid and executed to introduce Jesus to our posterity as the sin-pardoning Savior He is. With an intensity born of heaven, we must lead them in accepting Christ as their Lord and Savior and demonstrate to them daily what it means to live for Jesus in this sin-cursed world.

God designed Adventist education as a vehicle to lead our children into knowing Him personally as their Lord and Savior. Nothing short of an up-close and personal relationship with our young men and women will please Him. God yearns to have the same relationship with them as He has with adults. The following texts emphasize the importance of knowing God personally:

"And this is life eternal, that they might know thee the only true God, and Jesus Christ, whom thou hast sent" (John 17:3).

"And they that know thy name will put their trust in thee: for thou, LORD, hast not forsaken them that seek thee" (Psalms 9:10).

"The fear of the LORD is the beginning of wisdom: and the knowledge of the holy is understanding" (Proverbs 9:10).

"And to know the love of Christ, which passeth knowledge, that ye might be filled with all the fullness of God" (Ephesians 3:19).

As we labor prayerfully in providing our youth with a Christ-centered education, we cooperate with the Most High God to save our children and to bring to fulfillment the promises of God to fill this world with *His glory.*

Discussion Questions

1. How is Adventist education related to God's plan to have the whole world filled with His glory?
2. How is Satan seeking to thwart His plan?
3. What should parents, who want to send their children to Adventist schools but can't afford it or have no school in their town, do?

Changed: Inside Out, Top to Bottom

Babies are so precious. Our daughter was no exception when she was born. She was a genuine, bona fide cutie-patootie. She melted your heart with her angelic smile and twisted it around her little pinky within nanoseconds of meeting her. It was hard to imagine that in our precious bundle of joy lurked the seeds of sin. Once when her mother was breast-feeding her at six months of age, our little baby bit her mother's nipple and laughed. To stop this behavior, her mother gave her a little thump and told her, "No," rather firmly.

Alas, it was true for our daughter as it is for all humanity. "There is none righteous, no not one" (Romans 3:10). We are "born in sin and shaped in iniquity" (Psalms 51:5). "The heart is deceitful above all things …who can know it" (Jeremiah 17:9). We are as "an unclean thing, and all our righteousnesses are as filthy rags … and our iniquities, like the wind, have taken us away" (Isaiah 64:6). "All have sinned and come short of the glory of God" (Romans 3:23). In a word, we are messed up.

If the glory of the Lord is to fill the whole earth as He intends, then our descendants must be changed from how they naturally come to this earth. And only God can help them.

Goal of Adventist Education

God plans to restore this world to its Edenic glory and to fill it with inhabitants who serve Him unreservedly. Adventist education plays a vital role in God's scheme of redemption and restoration. God designed Adventist education to help *change* our children. The goal of Adventist education is to help our heirs become Christ-like and reflect the image of Jesus. But how does this happen? How does Adventist education work to change our young ones? What happens daily in a church school to bring about a change in the students' lives?

I believe the answer is found in the following text:

> "But we all, with open face beholding as in a glass the glory of the Lord, are changed into the same image from glory to glory, even as by the Spirit of the Lord" (2 Corinthians 3:18).

The praise team at the Shiloh Seventh-day Adventist Church in Little Rock, Arkansas, sang a song with these lyrical words: "I want to be like Jesus—just like Him!" Our boys and girls behold Jesus daily in all of their subjects as our teachers present Christ to them in all His beauty, glory, majesty, and winsomeness. They present Christ to the students as the sin-pardoning Savior and the mighty Redeemer. Our children see Jesus in all of His attractiveness—day by day, week by week, month by month, and year by year until their souls cry out, "I want to be like Jesus—just like Him!"

By Beholding We Become Changed

Method

> "But we all, *with open face beholding as in a glass the glory of the Lord*, are changed into the same image from glory to glory, even as by the Spirit of the Lord" (2 Corinthians 3:18).

Simply put, if you can't see Jesus, you can't be saved. If you can't behold Him, you can't be changed. God's method to change our youth is to have them behold Christ Jesus constantly. Didn't Jesus say, "And I, if I be lifted up from the earth, I will draw all men unto me" (John 12:32)? Didn't the Israelites have to look upon the brass serpent in the wilderness to be healed from their poisonous snakebites (Numbers

21:9)? The scriptures exhort us over and over to focus our eyes on God.

> "*Look unto me, and be ye saved*, all the ends of the earth: for I am God, and there is none else" (Isaiah 45:22).

> "The next day John seeth Jesus coming unto him, and saith, *Behold the Lamb of God*, which taketh away the sin of the world" (John 1:29).

> "*Looking unto Jesus the author and finisher of our faith;* who for the joy that was set before him endured the cross, despising the shame, and is set down at the right hand of the throne of God" (Hebrews 12:2).

"It is a law both of the intellectual and the spiritual nature that by beholding we become changed. The mind gradually adapts itself to the subjects upon which it is allowed to dwell. It becomes assimilated to that which it is accustomed to love and reverence. Man will never rise higher than his standard of purity or goodness or truth. If self is his loftiest ideal, he will never attain to anything more exalted. Rather, he will constantly sink lower and lower. The grace of God alone has power to exalt man. Left to himself, his course must inevitably be downward."[9]

The Lord has instructed parents to constantly present Him before their sons and daughters.

> "And these words, which I command thee this day, shall be in thine heart: And thou shalt teach them diligently unto thy children, and shalt talk of them *when thou sittest in thine house, and when thou walkest by the way, and when thou liest down, and when thou risest up.* And thou shalt bind them for a sign upon thine hand, and they shall be as frontlets between thine eyes. And thou shalt write them upon the posts of thy house, and on thy gates" (Deuteronomy 6:6–9).

Our youth are to behold Jesus 24–7. On the playground, they behold Him as a Friend that sticks closer than a brother. During lunch, they learn that He is the Bread of Life and that His Word is more precious than their necessary food. In English, they see Him as the Word—the Word that was in the beginning with God, and the Word that was God. In science, they discover that He is the Creator—the Designer of the universe. In math, they find Him to be the One who subtracts our sin, adds His righteousness, and multiplies His grace. Whatever the subject, our young people must see Jesus continually as the Desire of all Nations.

Metamorphosis

"But we all, with open face beholding as in a glass the glory of the Lord, *are changed into the same image from glory to glory*, even as by the Spirit of the Lord" (2 Corinthians 3:18).

Moses was shut in with the Lord for almost six weeks and did not eat bread or drink water as he enjoyed communing with the Life Giver Himself. At the end of his time with God on Mount Sinai, he descended from the mount unaware that his face was shining with a heavenly glow.

The same happens to our young people as they attend our church schools and behold Jesus all day, every day, and in various ways. Our young men and women are, by the grace of God, changed into His image *if* they do not resist and rebel against Him.

Our seed, as they behold Jesus, become Christ-like. They come to this world warped, twisted, and bent toward evil; but they become a new creation in Christ Jesus. They come sharing reluctantly; but they become unselfish. They come distorting the truth; but they become trustworthy. They come stealing and fighting; but they become peacemakers and respect the property of others because they are "changed into the same image."

And this is an ongoing change, according to 2 Corinthians 3:18. The Bible proclaims, "from glory to glory," which means that we are continually becoming more and more like Jesus every day. Moses' glory faded, but not so with us. Our walk with the Lord is to lead us into an ever increasing splendor.

Medium

The action of fallen human beings cannot produce the change that God wants our descendants to experience. Yes, our teachers teach the Bible and talk to the students about Jesus and the plan of salvation. But this alone is woefully insufficient to create the change needed to transform our sons and daughters into a new creation in Christ Jesus.

Note the last part of 2 Corinthians 3:18:

"But we all, with open face beholding as in a glass the glory of the Lord, are changed into the same image from glory to glory, *even as by the Spirit of the Lord.*"

God is the unseen Teacher and Helper in our classrooms by *His Spirit* to bring about this great change of heart, mind, motives, and purposes within our youth. A supernatural power works in our classrooms. Only God, by *His Holy Spirit*, changes a sinner to a saint and makes a new creation out of those born in sin and shaped in iniquity. Our schools must be bathed daily in prayer because we are engaged in a great spiritual battle for the souls of our young. We are doomed in our fight with the great adversary of our souls without God's presence, God's power, and *God's Spirit.*

The Lord longs to see our heirs saved. He longs to open up the windows of heaven and daily shower them with *His Spirit* as they come to Him in faith. Luke 11:13 gives us this amazing promise: "If ye then being evil, know how to give good gifts to your children, how much more will your heavenly Father give the *Holy Spirit* to them which ask Him?"

We can't change anyone. We don't possess that kind of power. But we can cooperate with One who can. As we do what He commands us to do and go forth in faith, we can rest assured that *His Spirit* assists our teachers as they seek to point our little ones to the sin-pardoning Savior. The *Holy Spirit,* the active agent and unseen Teacher in the classroom, removes the scales from the eyes of the students, breaks the enchanting spell of this world, reveals the everlasting love of a merciful heavenly Father, and saves our children.

Discussion Questions

1. What is the goal of Adventist education? How is this goal achieved?

2. What is the goal of public school education? How can public school hurt the spiritual development of our children?

3. Do you remember your church schools daily in your prayer? Why is this vitally necessary?

Walk This Way: The Path to Greatness

The United States of America is touted as being the lone superpower in the world today. Undoubtedly, it has achieved this status because of its military prowess. The United States spends more on its military than all other countries combined. In addition to being a military power, America's influence is felt the world over culturally, economically, and politically.

But what made America great? How did this relatively young nation rise to such prominence among well-established countries? What does this country have that other countries don't? I believe that the laws upon which this country was established played a huge role in catapulting this country to its present-day superpower status. Our Constitution and Bill of Rights were groundbreaking in the arena of governments when this country was founded in 1776.

But alas, did you know that there is another nation that God has ordained to be a superpower? And that nation is the Christian church according to 1 Peter 2:9. "But ye are a chosen generation, a royal priesthood, *an holy nation*, a peculiar people; that ye should shew forth the praises of him who hath called you out of darkness into his marvellous light." Originally the Lord planned to fulfill His promises of greatness to the nation of Israel, but they rejected Him. And now God transfers the fulfillment of these promises of greatness, prominence, and superiority to His church instead.

Consider just a few of these great and exceeding promises that God gave to the nation of Israel and is now seeking to fulfill in our lives:

"And the LORD *shall make thee the head,* and not the tail; and thou shalt be above only, and thou shalt not be beneath" (Deuteronomy 28:13).

"For thou art an holy people unto the LORD thy God: the LORD thy God hath *chosen thee to be a special people* unto himself, *above all people* that are upon the face of the earth" (Deuteronomy 7:6).

"The LORD thy God will *set thee on high above all nations of the earth:* And all these blessings shall come on thee, and overtake thee, if thou shalt hearken unto the voice of the LORD thy God" (Deuteronomy 28:1, 2).

"And it shall be to me a name of joy, a praise and *an honor before all the nations of the earth,* which shall hear all the good that I do unto them: and they shall fear and tremble for all the goodness and for all the prosperity that I procure unto it" (Jeremiah 33:9).

"And *all nations shall call you blessed:* for ye shall be a delightsome land, saith the LORD of hosts" (Malachi 3:12).

A Great Law

When we examine the previous texts, we see that the blessings and greatness that come to God's people are a direct result of obedience to His law. Hence, the path to greatness is through an intimate knowledge of God's law—the law echoed from the smoking mountain called Sinai, chiseled on tablets of stone by the very finger of God, placed inside the ark within the Holy of Holies, and distilled into two commandments by Jesus.

"Jesus said unto him, Thou shalt love the Lord thy God with all thy heart, and with all thy soul, and with all thy mind. This is the first and great commandment. And the second is like unto it, Thou shalt love thy neighbor as thyself. *On*

these two commandments hang all the law and the prophets"
(Matthew 22:37–40).

This law is summed up in one word: *love.*

"Whoever does not love does not know God, because
God is love" (1 John 4:8, NIV).

Since this law is from the Creator of the universe, it is the greatest
law known to humanity. It gives us the greatest and best path to travel
in order to please our Maker. By traveling the path outlined by the
law of God, we are enabled to achieve our highest possible potential.
No true greatness exists apart from the law of God. No greatness
of any eternal significance is possible for anyone who ignores the
commandments of God and refuses to obey them.

Seventh-day Adventist schools, academies, colleges, and
universities are uniquely situated to provide students (especially our
sons and daughters) with an education unattainable anywhere else.
Pupils can only receive a correct understanding of God's law, end-
time prophecy, the health laws, and the everlasting gospel as given
to us in the Bible at Seventh-day Adventist schools.

Many schools call themselves "Christian." Yet they do not teach
by precept and example that all of God's Ten Commandments are
still binding. All such schools have been "weighed in the balances
and found wanting" (Daniel 5:27). These "Christian" schools hurt
students by derailing them from the path of greatness either by
explicitly or implicitly teaching them that complete obedience to the
Ten Commandments isn't necessary.

Of course, boys and girls can find Jesus as their personal Savior in
other Christian schools. Christ can also be found in churches beside
Seventh-day Adventist churches. But does this mean that we should
patronize them to the detriment of our *own* schools and churches?
God forbid! On the contrary, the Bible is clear in Revelation 18:4
when it proclaims, "Come out of her my people." Earlier in this same
chapter of Revelation, the apostate church, called Babylon, is said to
be the "habitations of devils and the hold of every foul spirit." Does
this sound like a place to send our children? Is this the place that the

Almighty has designated for His children to be taught in order to bring glory and honor to Him and walk in the path of greatness?

The only reason Jesus is found in these schools and churches is because the overwhelming majority of sincere, born-again Christians are still in them. However, God is sending them a strong and unambiguous message that they are in the wrong place and need to come out so that they will not be partakers of this institution's sin. And where are they to go? To the remnant church referred to in Revelation 12:17, "which keep the commandments of God and have the testimony of Jesus."

Here are a few texts that point to the greatness of God's law and what it will do for those who keep it:

> "Behold, I have *taught you statutes and judgments,* even as the LORD my God commanded me, that ye should do so in the land whither ye go to possess it. Keep therefore and do them; for this is *your wisdom and your understanding in the sight of the nations,* which shall hear all these statutes, and say, Surely this great nation is a wise and understanding people. For what nation is there so great, who hath God so nigh unto them, as the LORD our God is in all things that we call upon him for? And what nation is there so great, that hath statutes and judgments so righteous as all this law, which I set before you this day?" (Deuteronomy 4:5–8).

> *"The law of the LORD is perfect,* converting the soul: the testimony of the LORD is sure, making wise the simple" (Psalms 19:7).

> *"More to be desired are they than gold,* yea, than much fine gold: sweeter also than honey and the honeycomb" (Psalms 19:10).

> "The law of thy mouth is *better unto me than thousands of gold and silver"* (Psalms 119:72).

> "Though despised by the Egyptians, the Israelites had been honored by God, in that they were singled out to be the depositaries of His law. In the special blessings and

privileges accorded them, they had pre-eminence among the nations, as the first-born son had among brothers."[10]

"From a race of slaves the Israelites had been exalted above all peoples to be the peculiar treasure of the King of kings. God had separated them from the world, that He might commit to them a sacred trust. He had made them the depositaries of His law, and He purposed, through them, to preserve among men the knowledge of Himself. Thus the light of heaven was to shine out to a world enshrouded in darkness, and a voice was to be heard appealing to all peoples to turn from their idolatry to serve the living God. If the Israelites would be true to their trust, they would become a power in the world. God would be their defense, and He would exalt them above all other nations. His light and truth would be revealed through them, and they would stand forth under His wise and holy rule as an example of the superiority of His worship over every form of idolatry."[11]

A Great Adherence to the Law: Follow that Law

Having a great law is not enough. Imagine a person who has a refrigerator and pantry full of food. Yet they starve to death because they don't eat the food that is readily available to them. We must do more than just admire this great law and extol its virtues to the world. We must also be vigilant and persistent in our obedience to this law. In order to travel the path to greatness, we need a great adherence to that law. Wishy-washy, half-hearted obedience to God's law will never do if we are to attain to the greatness that God places before us.

Pay close attention to the word *diligently* as it is used in the following verses:

"Only take heed to thyself, and keep thy soul *diligently*, lest thou forget the things which thine eyes have seen, and lest they depart from thy heart all the days of thy life: but teach them thy sons, and thy sons' sons" (Deuteronomy 4:9).

"And thou shalt teach them *diligently* unto thy children, and shalt talk of them when thou sittest in thine house, and when thou walkest by the way, and when thou liest down, and when thou risest up" (Deuteronomy 6:7).

"Ye shall *diligently* keep the commandments of the LORD your God, and his testimonies, and his statutes, which he hath commanded thee" (Deuteronomy 6:17).

"And it shall come to pass, if ye shall hearken *diligently* unto my commandments which I command you this day, to love the LORD your God, and to serve him with all your heart and with all your soul, That I will give you the rain of your land in his due season, the first rain and the latter rain, that thou mayest gather in thy corn, and thy wine, and thine oil" (Deuteronomy 11:13–14).

"For if ye shall *diligently* keep all these commandments which I command you, to do them, to love the LORD your God, to walk in all his ways, and to cleave unto him; Then will the LORD drive out all these nations from before you, and ye shall possess greater nations and mightier than yourselves" (Deuteronomy 11:22–23).

"And it shall come to pass, if thou shalt hearken *diligently* unto the voice of the LORD thy God, to observe and to do all his commandments which I command thee this day, that the LORD thy God will set thee on high above all nations of the earth" (Deuteronomy 28:1).

There are four different Hebrew words that are used for *diligently* in the verses above. In Deuteronomy 4:9, the Hebrew word *me'od*[12] is translated as *diligently*. *Me'od* means "vehemently" or "intensely." Just as one intensely pokes embers and blows upon a dying flame, we fan the flame of faith so that it may burn brightly in our children amid a sin-cursed and darkened world.

In Deuteronomy 6:7, the word translated as *diligently* is *shanan*[13] in Hebrew. *Shanan* means "to point, prick, pierce, or sharpen intensively." Sometimes kids are hardheaded, as my mother occasionally called her four babies. In order to teach someone who is hardheaded or has a thick skull, you have to figuratively pierce and prick their minds constantly.

The Hebrew word *shamar*[14] is translated as *diligently* in Deuteronomy 6:17 and Deuteronomy 11:22. *Shamar* means "to hedge about as with thorns, to guard, to protect, or to preserve." God entrusts something exceedingly precious to us when He gives us His law. The Psalmist asserts that the law of God is "more precious than gold, yea than much fine gold, and sweeter also than honey and the honeycomb" (Psalms 19:10). Because the law of God is so precious, we dare not handle it carelessly. We must do all within our power to keep it as the special treasure of our lives.

Lastly, we have the Hebrew word *shama*[15] which is also translated *diligently* in Deuteronomy 11:13 and 28:1. *Shama* means "to hear intelligently and to pay close attention to with intentions to obey." Years ago, an investment firm called E. F. Hutton had a very clever commercial. In many noisy scenes with people talking and minding their own business, someone in a private conversation would inevitably say, "Well, my broker is E. F. Hutton and he says ..." Immediately all noise ceased and everyone strained to hear what this broker had to say.

Indeed, when the God of the universe speaks and gives instructions, guidance, and directions, all noise should cease instantly. Let all the earth keep silent before Him and cling to every word that proceeds from the mouth of God.

God has given us the path to greatness, which is to walk within His great law. In addition, we greatly adhere to that law by listening intently to obey it, placing a hedge about it to protect it, pricking constantly the minds of our children to inculcate it, and stirring ourselves intensely so as not to let its importance grow dim in our lives.

"Their obedience to the law of God would make them marvels of prosperity before the nations of the world. He who could give them wisdom and skill in all cunning work would continue to be their teacher, and would ennoble and elevate them through obedience to His laws. If obedient, they would be preserved from the diseases that afflicted other nations, and would be blessed with vigor of intellect. The glory of God, His majesty and power, were to be revealed in all their prosperity. They were to be a kingdom of priests and princes. God furnished them with every facility for becoming the greatest nation on the earth."[16]

A Great Appreciation for the Lawgiver

Our students need one last ingredient to genuinely walk in the path of greatness: a great appreciation for the lawgiver. As they recognize what God has done in adopting them into the family of God, they daily grow in their love and admiration for their Creator and Redeemer.

The Lord anticipates having a mutual loving relationship with them. Doesn't the Bible say that "We love Him because He first loved us" (1 John 4:19)? He takes the initiative in showering us with His mighty love and waits anxiously for the first responses of a grateful heart. He repeats in His Word time and time again how He yearns for the love of His people and even requires it.

"Hear, O Israel: The LORD our God is one LORD: And *thou shalt love the LORD thy God* with all thine heart, and with all thy soul, and with all thy might" (Deuteronomy 6:4–5).

"And now, Israel, what doth the LORD thy God require of thee, but to fear the LORD thy God, to walk in all his ways, and *to love him,* and to serve the LORD thy God with all thy heart and with all thy soul" (Deuteronomy 10:12).

"And the LORD thy God will circumcise thine heart, and the heart of thy seed, *to love the LORD thy God* with all thine heart, and with all thy soul, that thou mayest live" (Deuteronomy 30:6).

"He that *loveth father or mother more than me is not worthy of me:* and he that loveth son or daughter more than me is not worthy of me" (Matthew 10:37).

"Thou shalt not hearken unto the words of that prophet, or that dreamer of dreams: for the LORD your God proveth you, *to know whether ye love the LORD your God* with all your heart and with all your soul" (Deuteronomy 13:3).

"Take good heed therefore unto yourselves, that *ye love the LORD your God"* (Joshua 23:11).

Our students learn that loving God is more than a rapture of emotion. Loving God is best shown by willingly obeying Him and seeking His will and pleasure in all of life's decisions. To say that we love God and then refuse to obey Him and walk in the path of His law is the height of hypocrisy. I like the way the NIV translates John 14:15: "If you love me, you *will* keep my commandments." The natural outgrowth of love and appreciation for our Creator and Redeemer is to obey Him. And why not? He knows the end from the beginning. He knows what is best for us and seeks only to bless us in all our ways.

God desires much more than a nominal love or appreciation from His redeemed creation. He entrusts us with a great law, expects us to greatly adhere to it, and longs to see within us a great appreciation for Him. The Psalmist proclaims, *"Great* is the Lord and *greatly* to be praised; and His *greatness* is unsearchable" (Psalms 145:3).

When we love God with all of our heart, all of our soul, all of our mind, and all of our strength, there is no room in our hearts and minds for rivals of any kind. That's why God has commanded us unquestionably to love Him so.

When our youth love the Lord like this, they choose to spend more time with Him—praying, studying His Word, meditating, etc. As they draw close to God, He draws closer to them. He bestows upon them wisdom and understanding. He guides their every footstep. Our children become modern day Daniels, Shadraches, Meshaches, and Abednegos. Our children will work in the highest offices of the land without compromise to their religious principles and their allegiance to the Most High God.

Why? Because they are on the path to greatness. They are walking in obedience to the laws of Jehovah, *diligently* obeying Him, and growing in their love for Him more and more each day.

Discussion Questions

1. How does God's law help someone to become great?

2. Do you believe that it is possible to be great in God's eyes while being ignorant of His laws or while ignoring or disobeying His laws?

3. If other Christian schools do not teach and honor God's laws as He commands, would it hurt our children to send them there?

4. What should parents do if they feel that the Adventist school is inferior to a nearby public school or a Christian school of another denomination? Would it be better to send their children to this other school even though they may teach error and destroy the faith of their children?

Checkmate: An Excellent Place to Find a Mate

The students gathered each Sabbath afternoon at Moran Hall on the campus of Oakwood College to receive final instructions for community outreach. Following Jesus' instruction, the students went out two by two. Somehow, Billy and Pansy were never on the same ministry team. Still, they became good friends. They talked often and shared their frustrations and joys with each other regularly. Billy became Pansy's campus brother.

After graduation, they kept in touch. When Pansy's engagement to someone else ended, she knew she had a friend in Billy and could share her sorrows with him. During one of their many conversations, they began to view each other in a totally different light. Instead of a friend, they now saw in each other a friend *and* partner for life. They married and established their home as one dedicated to serve Christ.

Heaven rejoiced on August 17, 1986, when Billy and Pansy were joined together in holy matrimony. Heaven declared a small victory in the great controversy between Christ and Satan because a Christian home is a lighthouse in this sin-darkened world, a beachhead in enemy territory, and a firm foothold on the slippery slopes of a secular and degenerate society.

Their union is no accident. The Lord designed our educational institutions as excellent places to find a mate. The Lord knows that a strong church begins with a man and a woman who are wholeheartedly dedicated to Him and to each other.

Everything hinges on the selection of the one with whom we link our destiny, even our eternal salvation.

"How much greater caution should be exercised in entering the marriage relation—a relation which affects future generations and the future life?"[17]

"It is from the marriage hour that many men and women date their success or failure in this life, and their hopes of the future life."[18]

"The believer thus makes a sacrifice for Christ which his conscience approves, and which shows that he values eternal life too highly to run the risk of losing it. He feels that it would be better to remain unmarried than to link his interest for life with one who chooses the world rather than Jesus and who would lead away from the cross of Christ ... This vow links the destinies of the two individuals with bonds which naught but the hand of death should sever."[19]

But where can one look for a good potential spouse? Has God given us any instructions or examples to follow in choosing a mate? Are there any pitfalls to avoid?

Biblical Examples and Admonitions

Early in the Bible, God highlights the importance of choosing the right mate in the story of the flood. Genesis 6:2 reads, "That the sons of God saw the daughters of men that they were fair; and they took them wives of all which they chose."

"The sons of God" are the descendants of the righteous, God-fearing people on the earth. "The daughters of men" are the descendants of those who reject the authority of God in their lives and live to please self. From this point onward, everything goes downhill. God declares that His Spirit will not always strive with humanity and the world is plunged into the depths of iniquity. God had no viable alternative but to destroy the world by a flood and start over again. The decision to marry outside the will of God marks the starting point for this horrific devastation and destruction. This dark time of earth's history emphatically underscores the seriousness of choosing a mate.

Abraham provides us with an example of the carefulness needed in choosing a mate, when he strictly instructs his servant, Eliezer, not to choose a woman of the Canaanites as a wife for his son, Isaac. In Genesis 24:2–3, Abraham has his eldest servant, Eliezer, swear by putting his hand under his thigh not to do this. Eliezer goes unto Abraham's home country, and by prayer and divine intervention, is led to Rebekah, a relative of Abraham. God smiled upon this union.

Again, the importance of marriage and mate selection continued to be emphasized through Isaac and Rebekah's offspring, Esau. He didn't make a good choice in choosing a wife—or in his case, *wives.* This was his first mistake. Esau was married to multiple wives at one time. To make matters worse, he married wives of the Canaanites and it is written in several places how this brought much grief to his parents (Genesis 26:35; 27:46; 28:8).

The above examples took place before anything was written by God to avoid these types of relationships. Evidently, Abraham and Isaac, because of their relationship with God, knew His will in this matter. Later, God explicitly and unequivocally commands His sons (and daughters) in several places in the Bible not to marry "strange women (or men)" (Exodus 34:16; Deuteronomy 7:3–4). The New Testament exhorts us in 2 Corinthians 6:14 to not be "unequally yoked together with unbelievers: for what fellowship hath righteousness with unrighteousness? And what communion hath light with darkness?"

Why is God so adamantly opposed to these marriages? It is because marriage to unbelievers or strange women/men will turn the hearts of God's children to serving other gods (Exodus 34:16; Deuteronomy 7:3–4). The Bible declares that all have sinned and come short of the glory of God. We have been born and shaped in iniquity. We don't need any encouragement from a spouse to walk contrary to the will of God. It's already in us to do that naturally. What we need from our spouse is encouragement to watch, fast, and pray that we enter not into temptation. We need them to pray for us and with us, to set a godly example, and to encourage us on our spiritual journey.

Unfortunately, we have far too much confidence in ourselves. We believe that we can stand against the wiles of the evil one in our own strength and transgress God's commands with impunity. In Nehemiah 13:26, Nehemiah asks the people if they are smarter or wiser than Solomon, the world's wisest king whom foreign women led away from God. Solomon was beloved of God. God communed with him, gave him wisdom above all others, and exalted him to be king of Israel. Still, after all of this, he succumbs to the wiles of worldly women. This is a bright flashing red neon sign screaming, "Warning! Warning! Warning!"

What does this have to do with Seventh-day Adventist Christian education? Everything!

Since the strength of our homes, churches, communities, and country is based on the strength of our individual families, our children must be taught the Bible and its teachings in regard to choosing the right mate. Parents must teach their children Biblical guidelines on marriage and have these truths reinforced by the church and the school.

Plus there is no better place to look for a future spouse than at our church schools, colleges, and universities. This is a once in a lifetime experience. In Adventist schools, students associate with many other young people of like faith for a long period of time. The likelihood of a repeat experience of this nature decreases dramatically after leaving our school system.

Of course, everyone in our schools is not converted and marriage material. It will still take much prayer and discernment on the part of the student to know if this is one with whom to link his or her destiny. Here is a tip for those who are looking for a spouse: start by only considering individuals who profess faith in Jesus Christ as Lord and Savior. Consider only those who are committed to love and obey Christ in all things as potential spouses. This is always a superior beginning point than no profession at all or worse yet a profession to live contrary to what the Bible teaches.

The Valuegenesis[20] study leads us to believe that those who are taught in our church schools have a greater likelihood of being lifelong members.[21] Hence, even if a person didn't find a mate in our schools, there is still the possibility of finding one in a Seventh-day Adventist church later in life.

Likewise, our children who are taught outside of our educational system do not understand our message as clearly as those taught within. They are more likely to dismiss this advice and marry outside the church. Then a generation is raised outside God's remnant church, without understanding the importance of obeying God in all things.

Once while making a pastoral visit, I asked the married couple when and where they met. There was an eerie silence. The wife was a member of the church and the husband was not. My question was never really answered and so I was left to assume that it was a place that the Lord did not approve—perhaps a nightclub, a singles' bar, or the like.

The world encourages singles to meet potential mates at museums, libraries, singles' bars, and nightclubs. I once saw an episode of *Oprah* where single women were encouraged to meet the men of their dreams at their local Home Depot store. I am certain there are many other places that are recommended as great spots to meet your future spouse. Nowadays, there is a plethora of dating sites on the Web and many couples have even met while working together at their jobs.

According to research by The Marriage Project, "The most likely way to find a future marriage partner is through an introduction by family, friends, or acquaintances." According to its large-scale national survey of sexuality, almost 60 percent of married people were introduced by family, friends, coworkers or other acquaintances. Furthermore, research states that the more similar people are in their values, backgrounds and life goals, the more likely they are to have successful marriages.[22]

But where is the best place for Seventh-day Adventist young people? Where is the ideal place for our youth? If you are a committed, single, Seventh-day Adventist young person, shouldn't you look for a life mate who has similar values, background, and life goals? Wouldn't that logically be a committed Seventh-day Adventist Christian?

There have been jokes that young ladies attend college to receive their *MRS* degree. In reality, Seventh-day Adventist colleges and universities are excellent places to look for spouses and to get that *MRS* degree.

Aquila and Priscilla

The Bible doesn't say where Aquila and Priscilla met. Nor does it tell us if they were already married before they became Christians or how they became Christians. But we know that they became a powerful witnessing team for Christ Jesus as a married couple. Aquila and Priscilla represent a model Christian couple.

Here was a couple who was willing to endure hardship for the cause of Christ and live by faith. They left their home in Rome and went to Corinth because of persecution of the Jews by Claudius. They became connected with the apostle Paul in Corinth and united with him to carry the gospel to the Gentiles. Though they had recently relocated to Corinth, they moved again and traveled to Ephesus to do missionary work.

They were bold and tactful in their witness for Jesus. When they heard Apollos preach boldly and eloquently in the synagogue, they were not intimidated by his gifts. They discreetly approached him and led him to a better understanding of the scriptures and to a saving knowledge of our Lord and Savior Jesus Christ. They were soul winners.

They were credible, trustworthy leaders in the early church. Aquila and Priscilla sent letters to Achaia recommending Apollos to the church there. He was well-received because of their recommendation. Apollos proved to be a great blessing to the church there and to the cause of Christ in the early church because of the influence of this married couple, who were wholly dedicated to the Lord. This couple had such an impact upon the early church that their names are mentioned in three books of the Bible: Acts, Romans, and 1 Corinthians. They were truly involved in team ministry. In every verse where one is mentioned, the other person is mentioned also.

If Aquila and Priscilla are models for Christian couples, where is the single Christian Seventh-day Adventist man or woman to meet such a mate? Is he or she to look on their jobs to those who do not hold similar values or beliefs as a mate for life? Should he or she look to Christians of other faiths to find that special someone to unite with in holy matrimony? No. In spite of the claims of some church members who maintain that they are in a satisfying marital relationship with someone of a different faith, the child of God should *never* enter into a marital relationship with someone other than a Seventh-day Adventist. The distinctive truths and beliefs we hold demand that we only unite with those of like faith. Then together we can witness to a dying world about a soon coming Savior who looks for a people who love Him enough to obey Him in every area of their lives.

Seventh-day Adventist schools are not the only place where Seventh-day Adventist young people can meet one another. Our young people meet potential mates at their churches, other Seventh-day Adventist churches, mission trips, youth federations, youth congresses, Bible Bowls, and Pathfinder events. The school and its various related events are only one among many venues for a Seventh-day Adventist young person to meet his or her potential mate. Nevertheless, it is probably one of the best of all the possibilities mentioned above since school affords an opportunity to observe a person under various circumstances and for a greater length of time.

Should dating be on our young people's minds? Do we send them to school to get involved with the opposite sex? I believe the answer to those questions is *No* for the children in high school and below. And *Yes* for those whose are college age and above. I know that some will disagree with me even for those who are older than eighteen. Whether we want them to think about the opposite sex or not, God has so wired us that, at a certain age, we begin to see the opposite sex differently. We find that they are attracted to us and we are to them. Of course, this is ripe ground for Satan to lead our children down a primrose path of destruction.

At some point in our children's lives, they will become acutely aware of the opposite sex and begin contemplating choosing a mate for life. As godly parents, we want our children to be committed Christians and members of the Seventh-day Adventist church. We also desire for them to understand the seriousness of marrying another committed Christian within the Seventh-day Adventist church and choose accordingly. The time when they are ready to make this all-important choice may be years after leaving a Seventh-day Adventist institution. Nevertheless, when the time comes, the myriad of friends and acquaintances encountered in Adventist schools and the other sources mentioned earlier provide a number of dedicated Seventh-day Adventist Christians from which to safely choose.

The summer of 1975 found Clifton and Venita on the campus of Oakwood College taking classes to ensure that they graduated on time the next school year. Until that time, they did not have a close friendship even though they had sung together in the Aeolians, a campus choir. Since fewer students were on campus, it afforded them an opportunity for greater interaction. The students especially looked forward to lunchtime when they took their sack lunches outside, sat on the grass, and ate under the trees.

Lively discussions and healthy exchanges took place during lunchtime that summer. Venita was not one to surrender her opinion easily. Clifton described her as "feisty" at the time. Once when their group was in the midst of a lively lunchtime discussion, Clifton jokingly picked up Venita and placed her in a trash can to temper her feistiness. But as time went by, Clifton became convinced that he had found in Venita a friendship and companionship that he never wanted to throw away.

Heaven celebrated as Clifton and Venita were united in holy wedlock on November 26, 1978. Their home became another beacon of light for Christ in a world darkened by sin. Adventist education had once again achieved a major purpose for which it was established.

Discussion Questions

1. Where do you believe is the best place for a child of God to meet his or her future mate?

2. Do you believe that your mate should be a Christian and a member of the Seventh-day Adventist church? Why or why not?

3. Where should Seventh-day Adventist young people who do not attend our church schools look for a mate?

4. What should be the overwhelming, driving criteria for selecting a suitable mate?

Passing the Baton: Training Leaders for the Next Generation

In his book, *Outliers,* Malcolm Gladwell describes how people become successful by application of the ten-thousand-hour rule. This rule states that we gain a proficiency that enables us to be among the elite of our field when we put ten thousand hours of practice and training into a hobby, sport, craft, or vocation.[23]

This concept of continual improvement through repetition and focused effort with proper guidance is nothing new to God. He wants our children to sleep, eat, drink, and breathe worshipping Him. So by the time they are adults, they have surpassed the ten-thousand-hour mark in worshippping and serving Him. They have an intimate acquaintance with Him, are knowledgeable of His laws and commandments, and are committed to His way, His will, and His mission. They have worked alongside veteran workers in God's cause and learned how to depend on God for success. They have a drive and passion for the things of God and for the expansion of His kingdom. They are ready and desirous to lead in God's work because of the training they received in Seventh-day Adventist educational institutions.

Again, let's revisit some key texts that speak of teaching our children.

"And these words, which I command thee this day, shall be in thine heart: And thou shalt teach them *diligently* unto thy children, and shalt talk of them when thou sittest in thine house, and when thou walkest by the way, and when thou liest down, and when thou risest up" (Deuteronomy 6:6–7).

"Only take heed to thyself, and keep thy soul *diligently*, lest thou forget the things which thine eyes have seen, and lest they depart from thy heart all the days of thy life: but teach them thy sons, and thy sons' sons; Specially the day that thou stoodest before the LORD thy God in Horeb, when the LORD said unto me, Gather me the people together, and I will make them hear my words, that they may learn to fear me all the days that they shall live upon the earth, and that they may teach their children" (Deuteronomy 4:9–10).

These verses speak of the diligence to be rendered in instructing our children in the ways of the Lord. So important is the transmission of the knowledge of the living God to our offspring that there is never an acceptable time for us not to teach them about the Lord. Even when we are not giving any actual verbal lessons, the very examples of our lives should proclaim His majesty and goodness.

Why are we to teach God's truth so diligently? First, so that our children have a personal, vibrant relationship with their Creator and Redeemer. Second, after having committed themselves totally to the Lord, they are now dedicated to carrying on God's work so that they eventually replace us in the positions we hold in God's church and institutions.

In ancient Israel, where were the priests, prophets, and kings to come from? All of these various workers and more emerged from the offspring of Israel. It was not in the plan of God to look to heathen people to come and lead in any of the affairs of Israel. Yes, foreigners could become leaders and workers in Israel if they embraced the God of Israel and became one with His people. Leaders are to come from among God's people.

God's institutions, churches, and schools do not operate on worldly principles. Leaders in our institutions need godly principles instilled in them and a passion for the work of God and the salvation of lost souls. They need to be born again, have a personal, intimate relationship with Jesus Christ, and a clear understanding of the history of the Seventh-day Adventist Church and our beliefs. They need to know prophecy, discern the times in which we live, and be able to give an answer to the world for the hope that they have in them.

God systematically provided leadership for the children of Israel from generation to generation. First, God appointed Levites by family to various tasks involving the sanctuary and its services. Thus, family members trained younger members to take over assignments when they became of age. Certain Levites offered the sacrifices while others were responsible for the moving of the sanctuary from place to place or providing music for worship. The training and transmission of responsibilities took place within the home school.

The Lord also used the apprenticeship method in training future leaders. Joshua served as an apprentice to Moses, which meant being his valet. In spite of the seemingly menial, mundane tasks, God trained and positioned Joshua to replace Moses as the next leader of the children of Israel. Elijah and Elisha had a similar relationship. Elisha was a servant to Elijah and became the next prophet to Israel succeeding Elijah. But before succeeding the prophet Elijah, Elisha completed an internship or apprenticeship under Elijah.

Additionally, God used schools to train leaders for His people. Under the inspiration of God, Samuel established the school of the prophets to counteract the downward influence in spirituality that permeated the nation. He trained spiritual leaders to keep the torch of faith burning ever brightly in the nation of Israel.

This work of developing leaders for the church is not to be done helter-skelter, hodgepodge, or left to chance. God has a plan and God has a method. God's plan is to begin the training of our young people in the home to serve and worship Him wholeheartedly. Next, we place them in school environments that nurture their faith. These institutions stress that the sole purpose of their existence is to glorify the Lord in every way possible.

As our youth seek to glorify their heavenly Father, they are taught to train their faculties to the utmost to be used in the service of God. As they discover their gifts and fine-tune their skills, they render service to one another and to the community at large. When they graduate from our schools, they are thereby infused with a sense of purpose and destiny. I admire Oakwood University's motto: "Enter to learn, Depart to Serve."

God trains leaders for the future with a strong bias for providing leaders for His work. Our publishing work, hospitals, churches, schools, universities, and community service organizations need leaders. Though our schools produce leaders to serve the church, they also generate leaders for the various segments of society so that the sweet aroma of Jesus is spread throughout the world.

Young Timothy

A great example of a young man who was trained and developed to carry on the gospel work is Timothy. Two books of the New Testament were written to him from the Apostle Paul: First and Second Timothy. Why do I say that Timothy was trained and developed to carry on the gospel work?

First, a holy mother and grandmother taught him to know the Word of God from his earliest years. The Bible says in 2 Timothy 3:15, "And that from a child thou hast known the holy scriptures, which are able to make thee wise unto salvation through faith which is in Christ Jesus." His knowledge of the Bible was more than intellectual. It was also experiential. Paul said of Timothy, "When I call to remembrance the unfeigned faith that is in thee, which dwelt first in thy grandmother Lois, and thy mother Eunice; and I am persuaded that in thee also" (2 Timothy 1:5). The great Apostle Paul discerned in young Timothy a sincere and genuine faith in Jesus and His Word.

Second, the apostle Paul mentored Timothy at a young age and persuaded him to become his traveling companion to help further the gospel work. Timothy took on huge responsibilities in pastoring a church while a youth. Paul encouraged him to not let anyone despise his youth and to be a model for others in word, in lifestyle, in love, in faith, and in purity (1 Timothy 4:12).

Third, Timothy knew the scriptures well enough to teach others in the faith. Second Timothy 2:2 states, "And the things that thou hast heard of me among many witnesses, the same commit thou to faithful men, who shall be able to teach others also."

Finally, while still a youth, Timothy endured hardness as a good soldier of Jesus and suffered for His sake. Timothy suffered as he traveled from place to place with Paul under crude modes of transportation and lodging. He faced imprisonment alongside Paul and harassment by those who rejected their message of salvation through Jesus. Furthermore, some in the church gave him a hard time because they did not take kindly to having a young man as their spiritual leader.

Still, Paul continued to teach Timothy by precept and example. Toward the end of Paul's sojourn on this earth, he encouraged Timothy with these words: "You have heard me teach others. You have seen how I have related to others and handled various situations. Now, you go and do likewise. God will help you and give you wisdom as He has me" (See 2 Timothy 2:1–3).

Discussion Questions

1. Do you agree with the author's premise that church schools facilitate the training of future leaders for our church? Why or why not?

2. What if a student has no desire to work for the church? Is this a sufficient reason not to attend a Seventh-day Adventist educational institution? Why or why not?

3. What are the advantages and disadvantages of having future workers for God's church totally trained in secular institutions for their entire lives?

The Four Church Schools

The First Church School:
Home of the Saved

I am a strong supporter and proponent of Seventh-day Adventist Christian education, or *church schools* as we call them. God calls for every child to attend church schools—all four of them. Let's take a look at the very first church school.

In order to have the *First Church School*, you must have *the first church*. The *first church* is located in our homes. Deuteronomy 6:9 says, "And thou shalt write them upon the posts of thy house, and on thy gates." Our house is God's house. Let's boldly and unashamedly broadcast it to the world so that none of our guests, neighbors, and friends has to guess whose side we are on. We are on the Lord's side.

What is the "them" referred to in Deuteronomy 6:9? If we go to the very first verses in this chapter, it is easy to see that "them" means the law of God.

"Now these are *the commandments, the statutes, and the judgments*, which the LORD your God commanded to teach you, that ye might do them in the land whither ye go to possess it: That thou mightest fear the LORD thy God, to keep all *his statutes and his commandments*, which I command thee, thou, and thy son, and thy son's son, all the days of thy life; and that thy days may be prolonged. Hear therefore, O Israel, and observe to do it; that it may be well with thee, and that ye may increase mightily, as the LORD God of thy fathers hath promised thee, in the land that floweth with milk and honey" (Deuteronomy 6:1–3).

The "them" in Deuteronomy 6:9 clearly refer to God's laws, commandments, statues, and judgments. The picture of God's laws inscribed upon the exterior of our dwellings evokes a picture of a holy place. *The home is the first church.* Prayers, hymns, spiritual songs, Bible studies, and joyous praises daily ascend to heaven from our humble abodes. Sadly, many get no satisfaction out of corporate church worship because they don't have *church* at home.

The word *church* comes from the Greek word *ekklessia,* which means, "called out ones." God has called us out of Egypt and Babylon. Egypt and Babylon are not to be in our homes. We are called out of false worship and confusion. Called out to worship the one true God. Called out to serve and obey the Creator God. Called out to be in the world, but not of the world.

The head of the home is the priest or the pastor of this church and has the responsibility to ensure that the home is also a place of worship. As the pastor, the head of the house schedules daily worship service in the home so that God's Word is studied, His name is glorified in praise and song, and His throne petitioned through prayer.

The home is not only the first church, but it is also the *First Church School.* God calls the parents to be the teachers in this church school. Of course, you can't teach what you don't know. Parents must become students of the Word to impart to their offspring the beautiful and wonderful words of life.

As teachers, parents must know the Word and live the Word. The consistent, godly examples of parents teach some of the greatest lessons children will learn.

"Our influence upon others depends not so much upon what we say, as upon what we are. Men may combat and defy our logic, they may resist our appeals; but a life of disinterested love is an argument they cannot gainsay. A consistent life, characterized by the meekness of Christ, is a power in the world."[24]

I did not grow up in a Seventh-day Adventist Christian home. I grew up in a home where adults occasionally consumed alcohol, smoked cigarettes, drank coffee, and spoke some choice, creative words. When my siblings and I attempted to imitate our adult role models in any of these forbidden realms, we were told, "Don't do as I do. Do as I say." This philosophy will never work in this school. In the *First Church School*, the teachers (parents) are living models for their students (sons and daughters). This is why the Bible commands us in Deuteronomy 6:8: "And thou shalt bind *them* for a sign upon thine hand, and they shall be as frontlets between thine eyes."

What's more, school is always in session—everywhere and at all times. We are seven days a week Christians—24–7 Christians. Class is always in session in the *First Church School*. Deuteronomy 6:7 puts it this way: "And thou shalt teach *them* diligently unto thy children, and shalt talk of them when thou sittest in thine house, and when thou walkest by the way, and when thou liest down, and when thou risest up."

As stated earlier, I did not grow up in a Seventh-day Adventist Christian home. And lest you get the wrong impression by some of the things that I am revealing, I did grow up in a very loving, caring home. I share the following illustrations to emphasize the point that there's never a time when parents are not teaching their little ones. The little eyes and ears are always watching and listening.

I remember going with my mother to the movie theater as a child around the age of seven or eight. Children, ages six and under, either got in free or at a discounted rate. The attendant asked my mother how old I was. She answered, "Six." What lesson was I just taught?

On another occasion when I was in my teens, I accompanied an uncle with his son and his son's friend to pick up furniture which my uncle had recently purchased. The store's manager directed us to drive to the rear of the store. As we finished loading the truck with my uncle's furniture, my older cousin and his friend knowingly continued to load other items which did not belong to them onto the truck with the knowledge and approval of my uncle. They kept loading until he finally had to say, "Enough, let's go." What lesson was I just taught?

How many families today are purchasing the latest movies, computer software, and music CDs from bootleggers in the presence of their children? My wife and I were giving Bible studies to a woman and her teenage son in Little Rock, Arkansas. One day during our visit, he proudly showcased their latest bootleg movie purchase, *The Passion of Christ*, without any sense of wrongdoing on their part.

Our unscrupulous conduct teaches our children that it pays to lie, cheat, steal, or disobey any of God's commandments. Beloved, the money we save by our ungodly examples is not worth the results we reap in our own lives and the lives of our children who imitate us.

The First Curriculum

The curriculum in the *First Church School* is *the Word of God.* We must teach our offspring the Word of God from their earliest years. The Word of God is so vital in training the next generation that they are taught God's Word from inception. I vividly remember the worship services we had with our unborn son and daughter. My wife and I sang children's songs and read Bible stories to them while they were still in the womb. So naturally we continued this practice after they were born.

There is a God and He has made Himself known through His Word, the Holy Bible. He instructs parents to *diligently* teach their young ones His Word. Teach them from the earliest age that the Bible is the most important book in the world. Teach them that this book introduces us to the Creator of the universe, the Lover of our souls, our Savior and Redeemer. Teach them the plan of salvation and encourage them to choose Christ as their Lord and Savior at an early age.

In this *First Church School*, the children not only learn scripture and become acquainted with the Author of the Word, they also learn the importance of obedience and service. They learn to obey their parents and others in authority as well as God. By the precept and example of parents, our sons and daughters also learn the joy of serving others and how to be a blessing in this world.

What are your children learning at home? Too many learn the wrong things. I heard a story about Cissy Houston, the mother of Whitney Houston. She expressed concern to Whitney about her daughter, Bobbi. Little Bobbi, only three or four years old, had learned to dance rather provocatively. Grandma Cissy thought something was definitely wrong. It was totally inappropriate for her granddaughter to be dancing in such a sexually suggestive manner at that age. But where did this young child learn such dance moves? Right in her very own home from her parents who were pop stars at the time.

A good friend once shared with me how his two-year-old girl tried to kiss him in the mouth with an open mouth kiss. Where did she learn such things? Sorry to say, she picked up this bad habit from watching soap operas.

God instituted the *First Church School* in our homes for our young ones to learn the right things, develop good habits, and be saved. The Bible says in Isaiah 54:13, "And all thy children shall be taught of the LORD; and great shall be the peace of thy children." I am appealing to all the readers of this book to view their home as a church and a school for their young ones.

The McCoy household was far from perfect. But we did do some things right as we raised our two little ones for the Lord. We established a family altar in our home and had regular family devotions. These precious times of family worship have given us many wonderful, cherished memories.

"It is in the home that the education of the child is to begin. Here is his first school. Here, with his parents as instructors, he is to learn the lessons that are to guide him throughout life—lessons of respect, obedience, reverence, self-control. The educational influences of the home are a decided power for good or for evil. They are in many respects silent and gradual, but if exerted on the right side, they become a far-reaching power for truth and righteousness. If the child is not instructed aright here, Satan will educate him through agencies of his choosing. How important, then, is the school in the home!"[25]

"The home is the child's first school, and it is here that the foundation should be laid for a life of service."[26]

Discussion Questions

1. What are you doing in your home that will designate it as a church school?

2. How knowledgeable are you of God's Word? Do you feel comfortable to teach your children the basics of the Bible? If not, what can you do to increase your knowledge of the Word?

3. What can parents do to make their homes a church school that meets the approval of heaven?

The Second Church School: An Institution of Higher Learning

Did you know that the church is like a school? The church is a place to learn about God, Jesus, the plan of salvation, heaven, hell, and a host of other things relating to God and His Word. This is why the *Second Church School* is *the Church itself.*

The Bible admonishes us in 2 Timothy 2:15 to study in order to show ourselves approved unto God as workmen that do not need to be ashamed because we rightly divide the Word of truth. Moreover, the church is referred to in 1 Timothy 3:15 as "the pillar and ground of truth."

Because we are determined to see our sons and daughters saved in God's kingdom, their presence in this *Second Church School* is indispensable. The church plays a vital part in their spiritual development.

Spiritual Warfare: A Battle for our Minds

Our babies are born into the middle of a warzone. If not literally, they are always born into a figurative one. The world tries to mold our precious babies into its ways, practices, and traditions. The world tells our kids that, "There is nothing wrong with sex before marriage." "If it feels good, do it." "It is all right for a man to marry a man and for a woman to marry a woman as long as they both love each other." "It's cool to pierce your body and get tattoos." Ad infinitum.

However, the Bible tells us in Romans 12:2, "And be not conformed to this world: but be ye transformed by the renewing of your mind, that ye may prove what is that good, and acceptable, and perfect, will of God." We are clearly in a battle for our minds. Should we allow this world to insidiously poison the minds of our offspring while we stand idly and helplessly by? God forbid!

Ignorance Kills

The Bible explicitly trumpets the dangers that accompany ignorance of His laws and ways. The prophet Hosea exclaims, "My people are destroyed for lack of knowledge: because thou hast rejected knowledge, I will also reject thee, that thou shalt be no priest to me: seeing thou hast forgotten the law of thy God, I will also forget thy children" (Hosea 4:6). And in Isaiah 5:13 it says, "Therefore my people are gone into captivity, because they have no knowledge: and their honorable men are famished, and their multitude dried up with thirst."

Since destruction, captivity, rejection, and famine await those who insist on being ignorant of the Most High God, it behooves us as Seventh-day Adventist Christians to pursue knowledge and wisdom at the feet of our Lord and Savior Jesus Christ. We know the dangers that await all who dwell in ignorance. We long for our young men and women to learn of the Lord and His ways that they may receive His blessings and not His curses. This is why we conduct the *First Church School* in our homes and make certain that our children are in attendance at the *Second Church School*, the Church, on a regular basis.

Jesus Had a Habit of Going to Church on the Sabbath

The word *Christian* means "Christ-like." As His followers, we desire to imitate Him and be like Him in every way. Luke 4:16 states, "And he came to Nazareth, where he had been brought up: and, *as his custom was*, he went into the synagogue on the Sabbath day, and stood up for to read." Jesus attended church regularly. This was important to Him and therefore it is important to us also.

Church attendance generates multiple benefits for church members. Some of these include making new friends, fellowshipping with old friends, enjoying beautiful music, worshipping with fellow believers, offering prayers for others, and having prayers offered for us. What's more, we are granted many opportunities to encourage others and to be encouraged, to work for the salvation of others, and to grow spiritually by using our spiritual gifts.

However, one of the major reasons to attend church regularly is to learn and grow in the knowledge of God and His Word. First and foremost, we strive to enter into the most intimate and personal relationship with Him humanly possible. As we attend church regularly, our objective is to personally know the Lord and everything about Him. Every time we come to church, we are prepared to learn, receive, and grow as if we were in school.

Teaching in Church was Important to Jesus

Note the following verses and how they highlight the importance that Jesus placed on teaching in church.

"And he *taught* in their synagogues, being glorified of all" (Luke 4:15).

"And came down to Capernaum, a city of Galilee, and *taught* them on the Sabbath days" (Luke 4:31).

"And it came to pass also on another Sabbath, that he entered into the synagogue and *taught*: and there was a man whose right hand was withered" (Luke 6:6).

"And he was *teaching* in one of the synagogues on the Sabbath" (Luke 13:10).

"And he *taught* daily in the temple. But the chief priests and the scribes and the chief of the people sought to destroy him" (Luke 19:47).

"And it came to pass, that on one of those days, as he *taught* the people in the temple, and preached the gospel, the chief priests and the scribes came upon him with the elders" (Luke 20:1).

One of my favorite verses that speaks of Jesus and His teaching is Luke 5:17: "And it came to pass on a certain day, as he was *teaching* … and the power of the Lord was present to heal them." Holy Ghost inspired teaching releases power and healing from heaven above. Every time we enter church, Christ has promised by His spirit to be present and to be the unseen teacher among us. Consequently, we can expect blessings from on high as we are taught of Him and by Him.

Jesus Often Called Teacher, Master, Rabbi

Throughout the Gospels, Jesus is repeatedly referred to as a "teacher." Sometimes He is called "Master" or "Rabbi" which is just a different way of saying "teacher."

"*Rabbi*, we know that thou art a teacher come from God" (John 3:2).

"Then Jesus turned, and saw them following, and saith unto them, What seek ye? They said unto him, *Rabbi*, (which is to say, being interpreted, *Master)* where dwellest thou?" (John 1:38).

"Nathanael answered and saith unto him, *Rabbi*, thou art the Son of God; thou art the King of Israel" (John 1:49).

"But be not ye called *Rabbi*: for one is your *Master,* even Christ; and all ye are brethren" (Matthew 23:8).

Teaching in Church Was Important to the Apostles

Following in the footsteps of Jesus, the early disciples and the apostles made teaching a prominent part of their ministry. Teaching was an integral part of the early church as the following verses show:

"And when they heard that, they entered into the temple early in the morning, *and taught*" (Acts 5:21).

"Then came one and told them, saying, Behold, the men whom ye put in prison are standing in the temple, *and teaching* the people" (Acts 5:25).

"And daily in the temple, and in every house, they *ceased not to teach* and preach Jesus Christ" (Acts 5:42).

"And it came to pass, that a whole year they assembled themselves with the church, and *taught* much people" (Acts 11:26).

Teaching was important to the early disciples because they realized that the church is an institution of higher learning. No other school on earth provides higher knowledge. In the church we learn about the Most High God, the Creator of all, the Sustainer of all, and the true origins of this earth and of the universe. In this place of worship we are taught about the origin of sin, the plan of salvation, the home of the saved, and the destiny of the wicked. Here is where we gain knowledge about the schemes of the adversary of our souls, victorious Christian living, good and evil angels, the aid of the Holy Spirit, and a host of other subjects. No wonder teaching was important to the apostles.

Teaching in Church Is Important to Us

Now that we understand that Jesus had a habit of attending church regularly and that teaching was important to him and the apostles, it's not difficult to see why teaching in the church is important to us also. The church is the *Second Church School* for our family. As members of God's church, we too have enrolled into this institution of higher and lifelong learning.

Regrettably, low attendance at Sabbath School indicates that the importance of teaching and learning has fallen upon hard times in many churches. What's more, a close inspection of those in attendance shows that many are not consistently studying their Sabbath School lessons on a daily basis. Such neglect of vital truths only weakens the church and its members.

However, when the teaching of God's Word is elevated to its proper status, corporately and individually, worship and fellowship imparts a life-giving knowledge to all age groups. This knowledge enables us to know the One whom we revere and adore on a personal, close, and intimate level. This type of an education is a life transforming activity. We come to church one way but we leave another way—more like Jesus! Now that's true education.

"And thou shalt *teach* them ordinances and laws, and shalt shew them the way wherein they must walk, and the work that they must do" (Exodus 18:20).

"Moreover as for me, God forbid that I should sin against the LORD in ceasing to pray for you: but I will *teach* you the good and the right way" (1 Samuel 12:23).

"We sustain a loss when we neglect the privilege of associating together to strengthen and encourage one another in the service of God. The truths of His Word lose their vividness and importance in our minds. Our hearts cease to be enlightened and aroused by their sanctifying influence, and we decline in spirituality."[27]

"Yet in the church I had rather speak five words with my understanding, that *by my voice I might teach others* also, than ten thousand words in an unknown tongue" (1 Corinthians 14:19).

"And the LORD said unto Moses, Come up to me into the mount, and be there: and I will give thee tables of stone, and a law, and commandments which I have written; *that thou mayest teach them*" (Exodus 24:12).

Discussion Questions

1. Do you go to Sabbath School? Do you study your Sabbath School lesson regularly?

2. What are we teaching our children if we rarely attend church or consistently come late?

3. Are you growing in your knowledge of God and His Word at your local church? What can you do to help improve the situation where you are, for yourself and for others?

The Third Church School: The School of the Prophets

Perhaps someone is thinking, "Surely we have enough church schools already! Certainly the first two church schools are sufficient to accomplish the plan of God for our children." Since this sentiment is not aligned with the will and plan of God, I respectfully disagree.

Close investigation of the Word of God discloses another educational system instituted by God. Let's call it the *Third Church School*. The *Third Church School* is literally a school operated by the church. In the prophet Samuel's day, these schools were known as the schools of the prophets and the students were referred to as the sons of the prophets.

The following passage from Ellen G. White's book *Education* aptly describes the conditions of Samuel's times and the need for this additional educational system.

"Fathers and mothers in Israel became indifferent to their obligation to God, indifferent to their obligation to their children. Through unfaithfulness in the home, and idolatrous influences without, many of the Hebrew youth received an education differing widely from that which God had planned for them. They learned the ways of the heathen.

"To meet this growing evil, God provided other agencies as an aid to parents in the work of education. From the earliest times, prophets had been recognized as teachers divinely appointed. In the highest sense the prophet was one who spoke by direct inspiration, communicating to the people the messages he had received from God. But the name was given also to those who, though not so directly inspired, were divinely called to instruct the people in the works and ways of God. For the training of such a class of teachers, Samuel, by the Lord's direction, established the schools of the prophets.

"These schools were intended to serve as a barrier against the wide-spreading corruption, to provide for the mental and spiritual welfare of the youth, and to promote the prosperity of the nation by furnishing it with men qualified to act in the fear of God as leaders and counselors. To this end, Samuel gathered companies of young men who were pious, intelligent, and studious. These were called the sons of the prophets. As they studied the Word and the works of God, His life-giving power quickened the energies of mind and soul, and the students received wisdom from above. The instructors were not only versed in divine truth, but had themselves enjoyed communion with God, and had received the special endowment of His Spirit. They had the respect and confidence of the people, both for learning and for piety. In Samuel's day there were two of these schools—one at Ramah, the home of the prophet, and the other at Kirjath-jearim. In later times others were established."[28]

Below are five additional reasons why the Lord would have us operate this *Third Church School* for our youth. I have extracted these from 2 Kings 2:1–25, which tells about the ascension of the prophet Elijah into heaven. Before he departs, he and Elisha visit the schools of the prophets one last time. From this narrative, in relation to our young people, we learn that God wants to do the following:

1.   Relate to Them

In 2 Kings 2:3, 5, 15, we read the recurring phrase, "the sons of the prophets." The tender term "son" is used for the students in this school. It conveys affection, attachment, and affiliation. The sons of the prophets are figuratively offspring of the prophets, those directly or indirectly inspired by God. The phrase "sons of the prophets" is really just another way of saying "children of God."

God directs us in this new millennium to order our home as the *First Church School*, our churches as the *Second Church School*, and to additionally operate church schools to educate our youth for earth and eternity because He wants to have a relationship with our children. His goal is to relate to our young men and women all the time, not just on Sabbath or at the mid-week prayer service.

God endeavors to nurture His relationship with our children and to deepen it on a daily basis. He cannot do this to the highest degree if they are sent to receive an education at the hands of those who do not serve Him and teach beliefs contrary to His Word.

We are servants of the Most High God. We are His representatives. The Lord longs for our heirs to also be His servants and representatives. Notice the intimate relation that God seeks to have with us as expressed in the following verses:

"If my people, which are called by *my name* ..."
(2 Chronicles 7:14).

"And they shall be my people, and *I will be their God* ..." (Jeremiah 32:38).

"For ye are bought with a price: therefore glorify God in your body, and in your spirit, *which are God's*"
(1 Corinthians 6:20).

"For thou art an *holy people unto the LORD* thy God: the LORD thy God hath chosen thee to be a special people unto himself, above all people that are upon the face of the earth" (Deuteronomy 7:6).

2.   Reveal to Them
Notice in 2 Kings 2:3, 5 that the sons of the prophet at Bethel and Jericho knew that Elijah would be taken away from them. Not only did they know this, but Elisha also knew this before they told him. "Unknown to Elijah, the revelation that he was to be translated had

been made known to his disciples in the schools of the prophets, and in particular to Elisha."[29]

How did Elisha and the sons of the prophets at Bethel and Jericho get advance notice on the translation of Elijah and by whom? We don't know how this news was communicated to them, but we do know that the source of the information was the Lord Himself. And why was this told to them? Because God not only wants to relate to His children, but He also wants to reveal to them "great and mighty things which they know not" (Jeremiah 33:3).

The prophet Amos tells us in Amos 3:7 that "Surely the Lord GOD will do nothing, but he revealeth his secret unto his servants the prophets." What a marvelous thought that the God of the universe will communicate with our progeny and share His secrets with them. Our offspring by divine arrangement are never to be in the dark about things that are happening and will happen on this earth.

"Declaring the end from the beginning, and from ancient times the things that are not yet done, saying, My counsel shall stand, and I will do all my pleasure" (Isaiah 46:10).

"Henceforth I call you not servants; for the servant knoweth not what his lord doeth: but I have called you friends; for all things that I have heard of my Father *I have made known unto you"* (John 15:15).

"He answered and said unto them, Because it is *given unto you to know the mysteries of the kingdom of heaven,* but to them it is not given" (Matthew 13:11).

"The secret of the LORD is with them that fear him; and he will shew them his covenant" (Psalms 25:14).

"But ye, brethren, are not in darkness, that that day should overtake you as a thief. *Ye are all the children of light,* and the children of the day: we are not of the night, nor of darkness" (1 Thessalonians 5:4–5).

"But *I would not have you to be ignorant,* brethren ..." (1 Thessalonians 4:13).

3.   Refine Them

In addition to relating to the sons of the prophets and revealing His secrets to them, God longs for them to reach their fullest potential through His grace and strength. God sees what they can become as they are refined through tests and trials.

2 Kings 2:16–18 clearly shows that the students enrolled at the Jericho School of the Prophets were not a finished product. They insisted on sending out a search team to look for the translated prophet Elijah in spite of instructions to the contrary by their new principal, Elisha. These young men kept on urging him until he was ashamed. Though students in this God-ordained school, they evidently had many lessons to learn. These lessons have a refining effect upon their characters and work to fashion them to resemble Jesus more and more.

Enrolling our children in church school, the modern-day school of the prophets, gives God additional opportunities to build a relationship with them and to reveal many things to them. Still, God has so much more for our children. They do not instantly sprout angel wings because they attend a church school. Our kids aren't perfect and neither are we. This Third Church School gives God opportunities to provide correction concerning wrong thoughts about Him and habits contrary to the Word of God. Here God assists parents in knocking the rough edges off their sons' and daughters' personalities and in polishing their characters to reflect His.

And why is this needed? Because we all (children included) are thoroughly corrupted as the following scriptures make plain:

"Behold, I was *shapen in iniquity*; and in sin did my mother conceive me" (Psalms 51:5).

"But we are *all as an unclean thing*, and all our righteousnesses are as filthy rags; and we all do fade as a leaf; and our iniquities, like the wind, have taken us away" (Isaiah 64:6).

"The heart is deceitful above all things, and desperately wicked: who can know it?" (Jeremiah 17:9).

"For *all have sinned,* and come short of the glory of God" (Romans 3:23).

"As it is written, *There is none righteous,* no, not one" (Romans 3:10).

"O wretched man that I am! who shall deliver me from the body of this death?" (Romans 7:24).

But praise the Lord, God intends to fix us (children included) in spite of the wretched condition He finds us in.

"I will *make a man more precious than fine gold;* even a man than the golden wedge of Ophir" (Isaiah 13:12).

"Behold, *I have refined thee,* but not with silver; I have chosen thee in the furnace of affliction" (Isaiah 48:10).

"But who may abide the day of his coming? and who shall stand when he appeareth? for he is like a refiner's fire, and like fuller's soap: And he shall sit as a refiner and purifier of silver: and *he shall purify the sons of Levi, and purge them as gold and silver,* that they may offer unto the LORD an offering in righteousness" (Malachi 3:2–3).

The amazing *good news* is that we are justified while we are being sanctified (or refined). And, if we stay in the process, we will one day be glorified.

4.   Rescue Them

A popular gospel song by Andrae Crouch says, "If I never had a problem, I'd never know that God could solve them, I'd never know what faith in my God could do." Living on planet earth means that we will encounter challenges and problems. Many will be beyond our ability to control or handle. Our boys and girls need to know that we serve a God who not only wants to relate to them, reveal things to them, and refine them, but who also wants to rescue them.

For this reason, He doesn't keep problems and difficult situations from them. God strives to build a strong faith in His children and a firm reliance upon Him, which can endure the most demanding circumstances.

In 2 Kings 2:19–22, the men of the city bring a problem to Elisha. They have a beautiful city, but the water is bitter and the ground is barren. To bring the problem to Elisha, the new principal for the school of the prophets, is equivalent to bringing it to God because Elisha is one of His representatives or ambassadors on earth. God inspires Elisha to instruct the people to bring him salt in a new jar. He pours it in the spring of the waters while pronouncing the healing that God has performed upon the spring and upon the land. Verse 22 states that the healing of the waters that took place that day is still present. Ain't that good news!

Yes, beloved! God wants to rescue us and use us to rescue others from disastrous predicaments. Our students must be taught and trained to take this message of hope to the world.

"Fear thou not; for I am with thee: be not dismayed; for I am thy God: *I will strengthen thee; yea, I will help thee;* yea, I will uphold thee with the right hand of my righteousness" (Isaiah 41:10).

"But *my God shall supply all your need* according to his riches in glory by Christ Jesus" (Philippians 4:19).

"So that we may boldly say, *The Lord is my helper,* and I will not fear what man shall do unto me" (Hebrews 13:6).

"The LORD is my shepherd; I shall not want" (Psalms 23:1).

Every child of God ought to be able to say in the worst conditions, "It makes no difference, whatever the problem, the circumstance, or the situation may be, because if I have Jesus then I already have the victory!"

5.   Restrain Evil in Them (and Use Them to Restrain Evil)

A very sad story closes the second chapter of 2 Kings: the loss of forty-two young lives—forty-two young people who didn't have to die young. Yet, they died a violent death at the hand of two angry she-bears. And what does this have to do with Adventist education? What is the connection between this story and the *Third Church School*?

One of the main purposes of church schools is to restrain evil on the face of this planet. First, God restrains evil through students who give their lives to our Lord and Savior Jesus Christ due to the influence of church school. The Lord curbs the tide of irreverence and disrespect among youth—initially by keeping church school students from being a part of this unruly crowd. They are taught a better way of life by precept and example. They are persuaded to choose the better way, the straight and narrow path that leads to life.

Second, God restrains evil by using the church school, its teachers and students, along with the rest of the church to be the salt of the earth to uplift the surrounding community to His glory. God holds back the tide of evil by using godly church school students to shine the light of truth in their homes and communities. As others see their good works, they glorify God, become more susceptible to the godly sorrow that leads to repentance, and at the very least feel enough shame to conceal their wicked activities.

In 2 Kings 2:23–25, we see forty-two idle children. They are not working, in school, or seeking to do anything productive in society. Along comes the man of God, Elisha. Someone gets the bright idea to heckle him. Evidently, the person thinks that this will make everybody laugh and make them look like a daredevil in everyone's eye. One person starts and everyone joins in mocking the appearance of this prophet of God and also the miraculous translation of the prophet Elijah into heaven. "Go on up, baldy! Up, up, and away Mr. Skinhead!" They were cracking themselves up. But their antics were far from funny.

Elisha turns and curses them in the name of the Almighty God whom he represents. Out of the woods come two angry she-bears that violently take the lives of forty two children. Not one escapes. Imagine the sadness that covered that town—the veil of gloom that overshadowed each home that lost a child that day. Had those young people been brought up in a home that believed in *Adventist* education, they likely would not have been torn to pieces by the she-bears. The chances of showing respect and not disdain for the man of God dramatically increases for young people who attend the *First Church School* in their home, the *Second Church School* at their church, and the *Third Church School* operated by the church. Why is this? Because God established church schools to restrain evil in our sons and daughters and to use them to restrain evil in society.

When evil is not restrained in our young people, we'll see some of the same actions as we saw in Elisha's day. Every now and then—to let the world know that He is God and that He is to be respected and feared—God has to have two she-bears come out and wreak havoc upon the disrespectful. Every now and then—an Ananias and Sapphira have to drop dead to let folks know not to lie to the Holy Ghost. Every now and then—the earth has to open up and swallow some people as it did in the days of Korah, Dathan, and Abiram. Every now and then—God has to spit on somebody to give them leprosy as He did Miriam to get the message out loud and clear: "I am God and besides me, there is none other."

The next time Elisha came to town, he was well received by young and old. Surely, he was the most respected man around.

Today, evil is running rampant in our society. The words of scripture are graphically being fulfilled before our very eyes. Second Timothy 3:13 states, "But evil men and seducers shall wax worse and worse, deceiving, and being deceived." If ever we needed Seventh-day Adventist Christian education for our children, it is now.

Discussion Questions

1. Does your local church operate a school? If not, is there one in the city or town where you live?

2. Are there enough children in the churches in your city to support the operation of a church school?

3. What can be done to provide the education that God wants for our children in your local church? Are you willing to make sacrifices to see this come to pass and succeed?

The Fourth Church School: Post-Graduate Study

We have come to the last of the church schools established by God for the education of His people. As a recap, the *First Church School* is the home. The *Second Church School* is the church. And the *Third Church School* is actually a school operated by the church for the education of its young people.

So where is the *Fourth Church School*? Who will be the teacher? What subjects will be taught? When will we enter into this school?

In the book titled *Education*, we find the following words: "In the highest sense the work of education and the work of redemption are one."[30] And in the book *Christian Education* we find this: "And the education begun in this life will be continued in the life to come. Day by day the wonderful works of God, the evidences of his wisdom and power in creating and sustaining the universe, the infinite mystery of love and wisdom in the plan of redemption, will open to the mind in new beauty."[31]

> "Heaven is a school; its field of study, the universe; its teacher, the Infinite One. A branch of this school was established in Eden; and, the plan of redemption accomplished, education will again be taken up in the Eden school."[32]

Where?

It is easy to see from the quotes above that the *Fourth Church School* begins in heaven. The Bible teaches that the righteous will be caught up to be with Jesus at His second coming. We will be with Christ in heaven for one thousand years (1 Thessalonians 4:16, 17; Revelation 20:6). And then we will change classes and return to earth to resume our lessons.

"I saw a new heaven and a new earth: for the first heaven and the first earth were passed away … And I John saw the Holy City, New Jerusalem, coming down from God out of heaven, prepared as a bride adorned for her husband" (Revelation 21:1, 2).

"For the *earth shall be filled with the knowledge of the glory of the LORD,* as the waters cover the sea" (Habakkuk 2:14).

"They shall not hurt nor destroy in all my holy mountain: for *the earth shall be full of the knowledge of the LORD,* as the waters cover the sea" (Isaiah 11:9).

Who?

Teacher

And who will teach us in eternity? None other than God Himself, the Creator of the ends of the earth, the Omnipotent One, the Omnipresent One, the Omniscient One, the Master Storyteller, the Master Illustrator—the Master.

We haven't been taught till we have been personally taught by Jesus. When Jesus taught on earth, the people stayed all day without complaining and without food. He positively stimulated and invigorated their minds as they stood or sat in His presence. The people had come to the Fount of all Wisdom and the Lifegiver Himself. They did not leave disappointed.

When Christ speaks, pearls of wisdom begin to fall:
- "The Kingdom of heaven is likened unto…"
- "What man of you having a hundred sheep…"

- "Behold, a sower went forth to sow..."
- "A certain man had two sons..."

Never before will people have experienced any teaching exactly like this. The Master Teacher will have to send us away after every class because we will never choose to leave His presence.

Students

The students in the *Fourth Church School* are the redeemed of all ages. All are "A" students. Scientists estimate that we only use approximately 10 percent of our brains. But in heaven we shall have the use of all of our brain power. It will be impossible to fail in the *Fourth Church School* because there will be no tree of the knowledge of good and evil.

"For now we see through a glass, darkly; but then face to face: now I know in part; but then *shall I know even as also I am known*" (1 Corinthians 13:8).

"For *this corruptible must put on incorruption,* and this mortal must put on immortality" (1 Corinthians 15:53).

"Who shall change our vile body, that it may be fashioned like unto his glorious body, according to the working whereby he is able even to subdue all things unto himself" (Philippians 3:21).

"Beloved, now are we the sons of God, and it doth not yet appear what we shall be: but we know that, when he shall appear, we *shall be like him;* for we shall see him as he is" (1 John 3:2).

What?

Subjects

And what shall the redeemed of all ages study in the *Fourth Church School* in heaven? Practically any subject imaginable. Below are just a few of the possible subjects for our enjoyment.

1. History – We can go beyond the history of this world and study about the origins of sin in heaven. In the *Fourth Church School*, the veil between the visible and the invisible world is drawn aside and wonderful things are revealed.

2. Science – Curious about the creation of this world or even the universe? We will study the records of creation and understand how God's spoken Word causes matter to appear.

3. Physical education – Adam and Eve had physical activity in the Garden of Eden. We also will exercise our bodies in this *Fourth Church School* as we "shall build houses and plant vineyards" (Isaiah 65:21).

4. Physiology and anatomy – The Bible declares in Psalms 139:14 that our bodies are fearfully and wonderfully made. As never before, we will delve into the mysteries of the human body and understand better the complexities that govern our physical being.

5. Music – B. B. King, Bobby Blue Bland, and other blues singers (assuming they make it to heaven) will have to get some new songs. There are no blues sung in heaven or notes of wailing and mourning in God's entire universe. Music is not one of my strengths. Nevertheless, I am looking forward to taking music lessons from the Lord Himself. Did you know that God sings? "The LORD thy God in the midst of thee is mighty; He will save, He will rejoice over thee with joy; He will rest in his love, *He will joy over thee with singing*" (Zephaniah 3:17).

6. Theology and the plan of salvation – "The science of redemption is the science of all sciences; the science that is the study of the angels and of all the intelligences of the unfallen worlds; the science that engages the attention of our Lord and Saviour; the science that enters into the purpose brooded in the mind of the Infinite—'kept in silence through times eternal' (Romans 16:25, R.V.); the science that will be the study of God's redeemed

throughout endless ages. This is the highest study in which *it is possible for man to engage.* As no other study can, it will quicken the mind and uplift the soul."[33]

"There every power will be developed, every capability increased. The grandest enterprises will be carried forward, the loftiest aspirations will be reached, the highest ambitions realized. And still there will arise new heights to surmount, new wonders to admire, new truths to comprehend, fresh objects to call forth the powers of body and mind and soul … All the treasures of the universe will be open to the study of God's children. With unutterable delight we shall enter into the joy and the wisdom of unfallen beings."[34]

When?

The *Fourth Church School* begins at the Second Coming of Jesus.

"For the Lord himself shall descend from heaven with a shout, with the voice of the archangel, and with the trump of God: and the dead in Christ shall rise first: Then we which are alive and remain *shall be caught up together with them in the clouds, to meet the Lord in the air:* and so shall we ever be with the Lord" (1 Thessalonians 4:16–17).

This is graduation time for the saints of God. Our caps and gowns are the white robes we receive along with the crowns for our heads. All will receive a doctorate degree – Doctor of Ministry (DMIN). Though we have received a terminal degree, all of us understand the vast knowledge that is beyond our present understanding and are committed to an eternal education program.

I began this book with an incident that happened while I was a student at the University of Louisville. I was scheduled to graduate in the spring of 1976 with a Bachelor of Science degree in electrical engineering. I missed graduation at U of L that spring because I wasn't ready. I did a lot of partying in those days and not enough studying. I stayed up late and many times I slept in class, if I even made it to class.

I attended the outdoor graduation ceremony and watched from a distance. The weather cooperated beautifully. The sky was clear. The sun beamed brightly as I sat on my ten-speed bike in the shadows of nearby trees and watched as friends with whom I had partied received their diplomas. Tears swelled my eyes as disappointment flooded my soul. Oh how foolish I had been to squander the few precious hours I had been given. I had pursued my own pleasure instead of the degree for which I was enrolled.

I am determined, by the grace of God, not to miss the graduation ceremony from this earth. By the mercy of God, I will not be a spectator in the shadows when Jesus comes again, but I will be a participant on heaven's grandstand who receives his diploma from the Master Teacher Himself.

Discussion Questions

1. What are you looking forward to studying in eternity?

2. Compare our future educational endeavors in heaven to your best educational experiences on earth.

3. How can we make the *Fourth Church School* real to our children, neighbors, relatives, and coworkers without being offensive?

My Personal Experience

The Miseducation of Terrell McCoy

Adventist education is vitally important in God's plan for the salvation of our children. Every born-again Christian parent should earnestly strive to give their loved ones every possible advantage of being taught of the Lord at every level. Our children are God's property and His top priority is to establish a personal relationship with them. This is why Seventh-day Adventist Christian schools exist. The Lord seeks to change the students in our schools into His image, lead them in the path of greatness, and one day use them to fill this world with His glory.

But what about those parents who did not understand the importance of an Adventist education and did not send their sons and daughters to Seventh-day Adventist church schools? Or maybe you came to the Lord after your kids were grown and they did not receive the benefit of being taught about the Lord. Is there any hope for these children? Are these children doomed to hellfire and damnation because of the ignorance or disobedience of their parents?

This chapter is written to give hope to those who have already raised their young ones apart from God's plan. My aim is to give hope to those whose children are grown and gone, and not give license to those who steadfastly refuse to follow God's instructions in this matter. Psalms 19:13 states, "Keep back thy servant also from presumptuous sins; let them not have dominion over me: then shall I be upright, and I shall be innocent from the great transgression."

Ironically, my first sixteen years of education took place in a public school setting. Strange, isn't it, that the author of a book such as this one is not the sole product of Adventist education? However, I'm uniquely certified to speak on the dangers of a secular education from an inside perspective. I'm also eminently qualified to speak on the hope that is in Christ for those who were miseducated as I was.

Public School Not *All* Bad

First of all, public school is not *all* bad. In Acts 7:22 we read, "And Moses was learned in all the wisdom of the Egyptians, and was mighty in words and deeds." Egypt was a mighty civilization. It was known for its architectural wonders, pyramids, sphinxes, mathematics, government, alphabet, and vast army. Egypt was the superpower of its day. The Bible suggests that the Egyptian education that Moses received made him a man who was mighty in words and deeds among the greatest minds on the planet.

Like Moses, I also received a good *Egyptian* education. I entered first grade at the Georgia Avenue Elementary School in Memphis, Tennessee, in 1960. Later, I transferred to Lincoln Elementary and Longview Elementary schools. I went on to attend Longview Junior High School and Southside High School. All these schools are located on the south side of Memphis.

In high school, I was a member of the National Honor Society, the Drama Club, and the Spanish Club; I was first runner-up to Mr. Southside; and I was president of the student body. I excelled in all of my classes, especially math. Because of my solid math background, I majored in electrical engineering at the University of Louisville. I graduated in December 1976 and relocated to Lexington, Kentucky, where I began working for General Electric as a manufacturing projects engineer.

With all of my accomplishments, public school appears to be as good as our church schools. Some may respond, "This is what we want for our kids—to get a good education and a job with a high income. If our young people learn to read, add, subtract, and do all the other things to help them become productive citizens, why is there all the fuss about sending them to Seventh-day Adventist schools?"

Public School Does Not Equip Us to Be Saved or to Save Others

The Bible categorically and unequivocally states that the wisdom of man is foolishness with God (1 Corinthians 1:18–25). Man's wisdom fails to accomplish the purposes of God. God's purpose for our youth is to be eternally saved in His Kingdom, reflect His image, and enjoy sweet communion with Him all of their days.

However, this was not the case in Egypt. The educational system of the Egyptians was designed to lead its students away from the true God. The Egyptians worshipped the forces of nature: the wind and water, the sun and moon. They worshipped the god of heaven, the god of the dead, the goddess of moisture, the goddess of the sky, the god of air and fertility—Osiris, Horus, Ra, Shu, Nephthys, Isis, Tefnut ... And they worshipped the pharaohs as god and created vast pyramids and temples in the pharaohs' honor and for their worship.

Moses, intoxicated with the miseducation of Egypt, sought to use his Egyptian military knowledge to liberate his people, but this was not God's way. Zechariah 4:6 states, "Not by might, nor by power, but by my spirit, saith the LORD of hosts."

In my miseducation, I was taught to pledge allegiance to the United States of America, but not to the God of the universe, the Creator of the ends of the earth. I was taught that the Bible is not true, that God didn't create the world in six days, and that humans evolved from a monkey. What's more, I was taught that there is no absolute moral standard to follow. I was taught to use my reason and intellect to establish what was right and wrong for me.

I was terribly miseducated to believe that it was all right to mingle with females in an unholy way. Throughout my years in public school, I attended school-sponsored sock hops, dances, and proms. I was taught to have sex responsibly and to use condoms. I saw so many pregnant teenage girls in high school that I became quite adept at detecting pregnancies at their very early stages, before it became widely known to others.

In spite of the havoc that alcohol wreaked in our community and the many teenage lives ended by it, I still was taught to drink alcohol. "Just drink responsibly," I was told. Since I began using my mind to reason and to establish standards for myself, it was easy to conclude that a better buzz or high came from marijuana and other illegal drugs. So alcohol for me became a gateway to other harmful drugs.

Evolution's theory of the survival of the fittest was drilled into me. This theory suggests that present-day species are here because only the strong survive. There is no place in our society for the weak. Here was a subtle way of teaching me to not love my fellow man.

Violence was a part of my daily life. During my sophomore year in high school, a fight erupted in a biology class. A student stabbed a classmate in the jugular vein. He died in the classroom. The next year, Sergeant Duncan, a Vietnam War veteran and ROTC instructor at our school, was stabbed at a talent show hosted by the school. Sergeant Duncan was acting as a chaperone and sponsor for this event. Fortunately, he survived this vicious attack.

Moreover, sports and athletes were treated as deserving of worship. I was taught by example that sports were vastly more important than the Sabbath. Friday nights and Saturdays were the prime times for football and basketball games and track meets.

When I finished my public education, yes, I had a good job! Yes, I made good money! But I was a mess! Seriously miseducated! Morally bankrupt! Spiritually dead! Hopelessly addicted to the lust of the flesh, the lust of the eyes, and the pride of life! Hell bound! Is this what we want for our sons and daughters?

Need for Reeducation

Yes, Moses had an excellent public school education. Nevertheless, God saw the need for him to be reeducated. Moses was unfit for the great work that God had planned for him to do. Moses needed to learn humility, patience, and trust in divine power. The Lord chose to reeducate Moses by having him serve as a shepherd of sheep for forty years. He was miseducated and had to be reeducated!

I too had to be reeducated. I had to unlearn some things that I learned in *Egypt!* I had to learn that:
- Might does not mean right.
- There is only one true God.
- People are not and can never be God.

- It is dangerous to lean to my own understanding. In all my ways, I need to acknowledge the Lord and He will direct my paths.
- There is a way that seems right unto a person, but the end leads to death.

Moses had to be reeducated. But, he wasn't the only one in the Bible. Rahab, a prostitute who worshipped heathen gods, had to be reeducated to know that the Lord is "God in heaven above and in earth beneath" (Joshua 2:11).

Ruth, a Moabite who also worshipped heathen gods, had to be reeducated. Afterward, she told her mother-in-law, "Thy people shall be my people, and thy God shall be my God" (Ruth 1:16).

Nebuchadnezzar, a Babylonian big shot, thought he was god. He had to be intensely reeducated. God's reeducation program required him to live as an animal on all fours for seven years. Nebuchadnezzar ate grass like the ox of the field and his back was wet with the dew of heaven until he completed his remedial course. "Who is the Sovereign Lord?" King Nebuchadnezzar declared. "He and He alone is the Most High and I praise and honor Him that lives for ever, whose dominion is an everlasting dominion, and His kingdom is from generation to generation" (Daniel 4:34).

If you have failed to provide your child with every possible benefit for his or her salvation, there is still hope. The Lord doesn't give up on us that easily.

God straightens up what's twisted up.

He cleans up what's messed up.

He brings down the proud.

He lifts up the humble. There is still hope!

He makes wise the simple.

He gives knowledge to those who have no understanding.

He gives to those who mourn—beauty for ashes, the oil of joy for mourning, and the garment of praise for the spirit of heaviness. There is still hope!

He gives power to the faint and to those who have no might, He increases their strength.

He shuts doors that no person can open.

He opens doors that no person can shut.

He saves the lost, rescues the perishing, cares for the dying, and snatches them from sin and the grave.

He gives life to those dead in trespasses and sins. There is still hope!

He turns sinners into saints.

He opens blind eyes, makes the deaf hear, the dumb sing, and the lame walk.

He restores the years the locust have eaten.

He opens the windows of heaven and pours out blessings so that there is not room enough to receive it.

And, He reeducates the miseducated. I know, because He did it for me!

Bibliography

Biblesoft's *New Exhaustive Strong's Numbers and Concordance with Expanded Greek-Hebrew Dictionary.* Copyright © 1994, 2003, 2006 Biblesoft, Inc. and International Bible Translators, Inc.

Committee on Public Education, 1998-1999. "Media Education." *American Academy of Pediatrics*, 1999, http://aappolicy. aappublications.org/cgi/content/full/pediatrics;104/2/341 (4 October 2010).

Committee on Public Education, 2000-2001. "Media Violence." *American Academy of Pediatrics*, 2001, http://aappolicy. aappublications.org/cgi/content/full/pediatrics;108/5/1222 (4 October 2010).

Dudley, Roger L. and Janet Leigh Kangas. "How Does Adventist Education Affect Youth Attitudes?" *Journal of Adventist Education* 52, no. 4 (1990): 24-28, 45-46.

Gladwell, Malcolm. *Outliers: The Story of Success.* New York: Little, Brown and Co., 2008.

Popenoe, David and Barbara Dafoe Whitehead. "Ten Important Research Findings On Marriage and Choosing a Marriage Partner: Helpful Facts for Young Adults." *The National*

Marriage Project, 2004, www.virginia.edu/marriageproject/
pdfs/pubTenThingsYoungAdults.pdf (31 August 2010).

"Violence in the Media – Psychologists Help Protect Children from
Harmful Effects." *American Psychological Association*,
www.apa.org/research/action/protect.aspx (4 October
2010).

White, Ellen G. *The Adventist Home.* Nashville: Southern Publishing
Association, 1952.
---. *Child Guidance.* Nashville: Southern Publishing Association,
1954.
---. *Christian Education.* Mountain View: Pacific Press, 1894.
---. *Christ Object Lessons.* Washington, D. C.: Review and Herald,
1900.
---. *The Desire of Ages.* Mountain View: Pacific Press, 1940.
---. *Education.* Mountain View: Pacific Press, 1952.
---. *The Great Controversy.* Mountain View: Pacific Press, 1911.
---. *The Ministry of Healing.* Mountain View: Pacific Press, 1890.
---. *Patriarchs andProphets.* Mountain View: Pacific Press, 1890.
---. *Prophets and Kings.* Mountain View: Pacific Press, 1917.
---. *Steps to Christ.* Washington, D. C.: Review and Herald, 1893.
---. *Testimonies for the Church Vol. 4.* Mountain View: Pacific Press,
1948.

Endnotes

1   Ellen G. White, *The Adventist Home* (Nashville, Tenn.: Southern
    Publishing Association, 1952), p. 159.
2   Ibid., p. 280.
3   The majority of Christian churches observe the first day of the week,
    Sunday, as "the Lord's day" when the fourth commandment of the
    Decalogue instructs us to "Remember the sabbath to keep it holy." See
    Exodus 20:8-11. Saturday is the seventh day of the week.
4   Ellen G. White, *Christ Object Lessons* (Washington, D. C.: Review
    and Herald, 1900), p. 195.
5   "Violence in the Media – Psychologists Help Protect Children from
    Harmful Effects," *American Psychological Association*, www.apa.org/
    research/action/protect.aspx (4 October 2010).
6   Committee on Public Education, 2000-2001, "Media Violence,"
    American Academy of Pediatrics, 2001, http://aappolicy.
    aappublications.org/cgi/content/full/pediatrics;108/5/1222 (4 October
    2010).
7   Committee on Public Education, 1998-1999, "Media Education,"
    American Academy of Pediatrics, 1999, http://aappolicy.
    aappublications.org/cgi/content/full/pediatrics;104/2/341   (4 October
    2010).
8   Ibid.
9   Ellen G. White, *The Great Controversy* (Mountain View, Calif.: Pacific
    Press, 1911), p. 555.
10 Ellen G. White, *Patriarchs andProphets* (Mountain View, Calif.: Pacific
    Press, 1890), p. 273.
11 Ibid., p. 314.
12 See OT 3966 in Biblesoft's *New Exhaustive Strong's Numbers and
    Concordance with Expanded Greek-Hebrew Dictionary*. Copyright ©
    1994, 2003, 2006 Biblesoft, Inc. and International Bible Translators,
    Inc.

Terrell McCoy

13   Ibid., OT 8150.
14   Ibid., OT 8104
15   Ibid., OT 8085
16   White, *Christ Object Lessons*, p. 288.
17   White, *The Adventist Home*, p. 72.
18   Ibid., p. 43.
19   Ellen G. White, *Testimonies for the Church* (Mountain View, Calif.: Pacific Press, 1948), vol. 4, p. 506.
20   Valuegenesis is a research study into the faith and values of young people attending Seventh-day Adventist high schools in North America in the areas of family, school, and church. The first survey was conducted in 1990 and another major survey was conducted in 2000. See http://en.wikipedia.org/wiki/Valuegenesis for more information.
21   Roger L. Dudley and Janet Leigh Kangas, "How Does Adventist Education Affect Youth Attitudes?," *Journal of Adventist Education* 52, no. 4 (1990): 28.
22   David Popenoe and Barbara Dafoe Whitehead, "Ten Important Research Findings On Marriage and Choosing a Marriage Partner: Helpful Facts for Young Adults," *The National Marriage Project*, 2004, www.virginia.edu/marriageproject/pdfs/pubTenThingsYoungAdults.pdf (31 August 2010).
23   Malcolm Gladwell, *Outliers: The Story of Success* (New York, New York: Little, Brown and Co., 2008), pp. 39, 40.
24   Ellen G. White, *The Desire of Ages* (Mountain View, Calif.: Pacific Press, 1940), pp. 141,142.
25   Ellen G. White, *Child Guidance* (Nashville, Tenn.: Southern Publishing Association, 1954), p. 17.
26   Ellen G. White, *The Ministry of Healing* (Mountain View, Calif.: Pacific Press, 1890), p. 400.
27   Ellen G. White, *Steps to Christ* (Washington, D. C.: Review and Herald, 1893), p. 101.
28   Ellen G. White, *Education* (Mountain View, Calif.: Pacific Press, 1952), pp. 45, 46.
29   Ellen G. White, *Prophets and Kings* (Mountain View, Calif.: Pacific Press, 1917), p. 225.
30   White, *Education*, p. 30.
31   Ellen G. White, *Christian Education* (Mountain View, Calif.: Pacific Press, 1894), p. 70.
32   White, *Education*, p. 301.
33   Ibid., p. 126.
34   Ibid., p. 307.